The Living Journal
A Way Toward Freedom in the Service of Life

Christian Koontz, RSM

Sheed & Ward

Dedication

For my family and friends,
with profound respect, affection, and gratitude

Sheed & Ward™ is a service of National Catholic Reporter Publishing Company, Inc.

Library of Congress Card Number: 90-62087

ISBN: 1-55612-370-1

Published by: Sheed & Ward
115 E. Armour Blvd. P.O. Box 419492
Kansas City, MO 64141-6492

To order, call: (800) 333-7373

Contents

Acknowledgments

I am grateful to Mercy College of Detroit and the Sisters of Mercy of Erie, Pennsylvania, for graciously granting me a sabbatical leave for calendar year 1988 to write.

My thanks to the sponsors and participants in Living Journal workshops. I am especially grateful to those who have shared their experience and reflections with me. Thanks, too, to those persons who read and critiqued parts of this manuscript, including Susan Lombardi; Rita Panciera, RSM; Rose Ann Trzil, OSF; and to the staff of Mercy College of Detroit, especially Betty Szalay and Irene Cegielka for research assistance, and Emmy Yousey, for the illustrations. Special thanks to JoAnne Isbey, who takes the risks to support the creative wherever she finds it.

Preface

By 1985, the moves of the Living Journal presented here had begun to emerge out of my own experience. I soon began to teach aspects of the Journal in formal college English courses and in workshops with persons from a wide variety of backgrounds, interests, and needs.

The Living Journal can be a journal for living in process. As such, it is a tool or a vehicle for evoking the inner life. We have only to step into it and let it carry us where the Spirit of Life which is Ultimate Mystery wishes to go. The more we use it, the more it becomes a *living* journal, a carrier of the "pulsing flow" and continuity of our life.

Many persons have indicated that the simple structure and integrated series of moves of the Living Journal have a "peculiar power" to enrich their lives. They can use it as much or as little as they like, adapt it to their own needs and desires, and use it alone or in conjunction with other methods of inner work, such as spiritual direction, Jungian analysis, or Twelve Step programs. This response prompts me to publish the basic moves of the Living Journal to a wider audience.

The Living Journal will probably be most helpful to persons who long for genuine interior freedom and those haunted by the question, "Is this all there is?" Such persons sense that, contrary to prevailing opinion, genuinely human life is not about winning and losing, success and failure, getting and spending, having and not having. Truly human life is about learning and growing and changing. It is about allowing ourselves to be transformed through our relationships with ourselves, other persons, our works, the environment, and our God, however we name or understand God. It is about living the truth in love. It is about becoming free in the service of all life.

The Living Journal is a process that can enable that growth toward freedom. It can help us to move through dualism, dishonesty, and control, which Ann Wilson Schaef calls the three "perilous processes" within the addictive system (1987). The Living Journal can help us to go deeper within ourselves and gain access to our most profound wisdom and greatest energy for living a more authentic human life.

The Spirit of Life which is Ultimate Mystery calls each of us to undertake this journey into the wilderness in search of the Holy Grail. Life promises and delivers a wine ever more flowing and refreshing to those who commit themselves to that journey and remain faithful to it to the end. Let us trust ourselves to the Spirit of Life, then, and plunge into the work of the Living Journal.

Introduction

Two basic processes are in constant dialectic within the universe: the processes of creating and healing. Through entering into the creative process we make of ourselves and our world what they are. In the making we are often diminished and wounded, and we suffer loss, so we find ourselves constantly in need of healing.

Both creating and healing, if they are to be authentic and effective in the long run, must flow from the depths beyond all doctrines, the depth of the Spirit, the divine spark within us. Both creating and healing engage us in a dialectical movement between these depths and the surface, gradually loosening and raising the contents of consciousness from the depths where they are hidden and objectifying them on the surface of consciousness.

If the present Age of Destruction is to give way to a new Age of Creation more and more of us must commit ourselves to a profound engagement with creative and healing processes. Many modern persons are discovering the hidden power of writing as an aid to creativity and healing. The Living Journal is one way to unleash that power.

To be real and effective, Journal work must be rooted in the concrete, nitty-gritty facts of our daily lives. As Bernard Lonergan puts it, "What is good, always is concrete" (p. 27). Through six basic Journal moves we can gather the facts presently moving in our lives, pay careful attention to them, and integrate them more profoundly into our consciousness.

Method

After a brief overview of these six moves we will look at how to set up a Living Journal notebook and some general guidelines for Journal work. Then we will move, chapter by chapter, through the six moves, considering the purpose and procedures for each move, then making the moves, one by one. Each chapter ends with some excursions and ruminations which are just that, forays into the wilderness in search of nourishment and light.

Those who have some experience with inner work may need little explanation and may want to get right into the flow of the moves. If so, they may simply read the purposes, procedures, and making the move sections of each chapter, reserving the excursions and ruminations for another time.

On the other hand, those who do not have much experience with inner work may find the reflections helpful in orienting them to the work, motivating them to undertake the discipline required, or supporting and sustaining them in the work.

Chapter 7 consists of suggestions for expanding and deepening these six basic moves. The conclusion addresses several issues relevant to Living Journal theory and practice.

An Overview of the Six Basic Moves

The six basic moves of the Living Journal include: 1) establishing the appropriate atmosphere; 2) focusing, jotting, and brainstreaming; 3) keywording with response; 4) indexing with response; 5) clustering; and 6) deciding.

In the first move, we take a few moments to create an atmosphere of quiet and stillness which enables us to center ourselves. When we feel ready, we begin the second move, gathering relevant facts of our lives through focusing, jotting, and brainstreaming. In focusing, we center our attention on just how we find ourselves in the present moment. Once centered and focused on the work at hand, we jot down whatever bits and pieces of memory, imagery, feeling, and thought we find moving within us. If a bit or a piece "takes off," seemingly with a life of its own, we brainstream, allowing the fragment to spin itself out until our writing comes spontaneously to a close.

We "clear the buffer," so to speak, by focusing our attention on the present moment and centering ourselves within this present moment. From this centered position we continue to gather those images, feelings, questions, memories, and fragments that we find to be touching us and moving within us at the moment of writing.

Through the third move, keywording with response, we name that which is touching and moving us and allow it to extend itself and deepen. As we keyword and respond to our initial writing, still more facts associated with those that came through the initial brainstreaming are stirred up and brought to the surface of our consciousness. Like a second wind in running or swimming, this response move often draws from a deeper level of consciousness than that with which we began focusing, jotting, and brainstreaming.

The fourth move, indexing with response, helps to identify what we have written, and evokes still more data from a deeper level, and integrates that data more thoroughly. Indexing also prompts us to the fifth move, clustering.

Clustering, the fifth move, can help us to become more conscious of what is seeking to be brought to greater awareness, to be more fully resolved, or to be externalized in action. Clustering can also help us to clarify the data of our experience, understand it better, and determine its meaning and value.

The sixth move, deciding, helps us to discern the source and direction of our inner movements so that we can act on them more freely, appropriately, and fruitfully.

Underlying Principle

Underlying these six basic Journal moves is a fundamental operating principle which flows from the nature of the creative process, the principle of progressive and recursive deepening and broadening. Through the interplay of these six moves we evoke an inner memory, image, question, feeling, or idea; allow it to spin itself out as far as it can go; double back to allow it to penetrate still deeper; and then let it spiral out again even more deeply and broadly. If followed in appropriate rhythm and balance, these six moves can help us to integrate our experience into our consciousness, draw our lives into focus, and evoke greater energy and a clearer sense of direction for the future.

As in learning to do anything, we may find ourselves a little mechanical and awkward at first in carrying out these moves. With experience, however, we can enter more and more freely into this progressive and recursive spiral of life and flow gently and appropriately from one move to another, in a rhythm and balance most natural to us. As we do that, we discover that we are neither flotsam and jetsam battered about on the sea of life nor barges being hauled inexorably toward a predetermined destiny. Rather, we are like graceful sailboats, able to steer our own course in harmony with the other ships sailing the winds and currents of the sea.

Setting Up a Living Journal Notebook

The work of these moves is carried out in a simply designed notebook. The size and quality of the notebook can vary according to our personal taste, and a number of options may be added. Many persons find that an 8 1/2" x 11" three-ring, looseleaf binder is practical, convenient, and easily obtained. Others find the easy portability of a 6" x 9" notebook helpful. Whatever size, quality, and color we choose, it is important that our choice of notebook help motivate us to use it and do honor to the life that it will evoke and carry within its pages.

We place a sheaf of notebook paper, lined or unlined, whichever we prefer, in the notebook and draw a margin parallel to the outside vertical edge of each page and about two inches from it. We will do most of our Journal writing in the wider section of the page to the left.

The narrower section to the right, called the "Keyword Margin," has a special function which will be explained in Chapter 3. If we choose to write on both sides of the page, we should be sure that the Keyword Margin is always on the outer edge, to ensure ease of later reference. We number the pages on the bottom in the Keyword Margin:

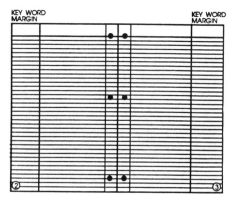

Once we have prepared the pages for writing, we place an alphabetical index at the back of the notebook behind the sheaf of paper. We also insert a sheet of paper behind each letter of the alphabet:

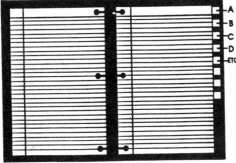

As our work unfolds, we may find that some options may facilitate and enrich our Journal work. For example, we may wish to insert copies of letters we have received and our responses to them right into our Journal on the date we respond. Or we may wish to respond in our Journal to an article we have read and then file the article right in the Journal along with our response. If so, we can insert pockets to hold these materials—or punch them with a three-hole punch. The principle is, it is our Journal, so we make it our own and use it as we like.

Place and Time for Journal Work

Journal work can be done almost anywhere, at almost any time. We find the place and time that are most possible for us to relax, meditate, and write freely without disturbance. We may want to set aside a place and a time and tell family and friends that this is a time for ourselves, a time when we are not to be disturbed. This may take some experimentation. As we interiorize the Journal moves, we will find that we are more and more able to take advantage of even a little space of time that may be available to us, whatever our outward circumstances.

For some, writing first thing in the morning is most helpful. It seems that sleep cleanses their consciousness and frees the inner flow. Also, when they have not yet been involved in the day's activities they can often give themselves more freely to their Journal work. Early morning writing also helps to center them and orient them to the day's activities and responsibilities.

For others, writing at night, just before retiring, is a good way to prepare for sleep. With the day's responsibilities met, they can relax more readily, clear the buffer, and allow themselves to descend into the depths. Free of the press of other responsibilities, they can devote themselves to their Journal work with a single heart.

For some, it may be that the nature and structure of the work day provide some other more congenial space and more opportune time for meditative writing. They may be able, for example, to arrive half an hour early for work or set aside half an hour of the lunch period or stop at a library, on occasion, on the way home from work.

We can also keep our Journal—or some of its pages—with us as we go about our business. Having it with us at meetings or other appointments, we can sometimes take advantage of unexpected "waiting" time for doing our Journal work.

General Guidelines

The inward journey is one each of us must undertake alone yet we cannot go inward alone. The wise think twice before they embark on the inward journey, and they do not go unprepared into the unknown. In the early stages, especially, but throughout the journey, we need the guidance, support, and affirmation of others as we open ourselves to darkness, not only the darkness of our own human condition in particular but also the darkness of the human condition in general. It is best to travel, then, in company with others, either in a group of like-spirited persons or with the guidance of an experienced traveler.

Perhaps the most important guideline for Journal work is that we be as gentle, free, accepting, and trusting as possible with ourselves. In the company of our Journal, we are simply present to ourselves, however we are at the moment, without judging or criticizing how we are. Nothing is to be forced; everything is allowed to happen when and how and if it will. If nothing seems to be happening, that is all right, too.

Often when we think nothing is happening, as May Sarton's poem puts it, "Something is stacking up to happen." Our work at such times is to be still and wait. We make no demands, have no expectations. We are simply available for recording whatever is touching or moving us at the moment of writing, without judgment, without criticism, without censorship.

At the moment of writing, we alone are the audience for what we write. If there is reason, we may later choose to share what we have written with another. The Journal may be used, for example, in conjunction with therapy or spiritual direction or group prayer and study, but we alone decide what we will share and when and with whom.

As we do our Journal work, we pay close attention to our body and obey its signals. If we are tired, we rest. If we are hungry, we eat. If we are restless, we walk. At times we will find ourselves uncomfortable at what our work is revealing to us. If so, we acknowledge our discomfort and do whatever we need to do to be in the discomfort and moved through it. If we are unduly afraid, or if we find that our Journal work unnerves us or disturbs us, then of course we seek the help of a counselor or a wise friend.

A Living Journal session is much like a physical workout. However brief, each session should provide a transition to move us gently into the work of the session and a gentle transition preparing us for the activities to follow the Journal session: we warm up before our inner workout; we concentrate on the workout; and we cool down after it.

If we have been upset before writing, for example, we take a few moments to calm ourselves down. If we are tired, we take a few moments to rest. Once we have centered ourselves for the work ahead, we make the recommended Journal move or moves. Before going on to other activities that await us, we bring our Journal work to closure. This closure turns the focus of our attention from the inner flow to outer events, reorienting us to other responsibilities which we can now undertake out of a more profoundly centered self. Often this closure may take the form of a brief rest or a to-do list which reorients us to external reality and guides our action in the immediate time ahead.

In the beginning of Journal work it is a helpful practice to make a commitment to "work out," as Roosevelt McCoy puts it, in the Journal every day for two or three weeks. In this way, we take full advantage of the learning and forgetting curve. (Research indicates that we tend to forget most rapidly immediately after learning something. Reviewing material within twenty-four hours after learning it and then within two or three weeks seems to retard the forgetting process most effectively. See Walter Pauk, (1984). *How to Study in College.* 3rd. Ed. Boston: Houghton.) At the end of the two or three weeks we should have a good indication of whether or not this approach to Journal work is congenial and helpful for us to continue.

Chapter 1

The First Move:
Establishing the Appropriate
Atmosphere

Before we begin our Journal work, we need to establish both within and without an appropriate atmosphere, an atmosphere conducive to relaxing, concentrating our attention on the inner world, and quieting the cacophony of voices within us. This need not be an elaborate nor time-consuming ritual. With experience, the atmosphere can be established very simply in just a few minutes. We simply take a few moments to find and prepare an appropriate place for our work and quiet ourselves, in whatever ways are comfortable for us.

Purpose

As we establish the appropriate atmosphere, we shift our inner gears and make a smooth transition from what we were doing to what we are going to do now, in the moments ahead. We begin to center ourselves, gathering our thoughts and feelings together so that we can focus our attention on the work that faces us. We pull ourselves together and shift the focus of our attention from outer reality to inner reality.

This kind of centering can help us close one frame of mind and heart and open us to another, more appropriate for the experience at hand. It clears the buffer, so to speak, and settles us in to the work now at hand.

We can learn to do this all the time, even outside the Journal exercises, just by taking a few moments to recollect ourselves, making ourselves more consciously aware of just where we are and just what we are about to do.

Procedures

To establish an appropriate atmosphere for inner work, we use any aids and rituals that are comfortable and helpful for us. For example, we may have a favorite setting where we find it easy to relax and center ourselves. We may have a favorite chair with a special view that we find conducive to meditation. Or perhaps we have some *objet d'art*, a painting or a small sculpture, or a flowering plant that helps to create such an atmosphere. We may also find it helpful to light a candle, being mindful of the quiet time ahead.

Making the Move

Once we have established ourselves in an environment conducive to quiet, we settle in to a position comfortable for us to relax and write. We sit quietly for a few moments, considering what we are about and centering our attention on the work ahead. Let us take a few moments, then, to relax and allow ourselves to be drawn into a meditative atmosphere. We may find the following Opening Meditation helpful in doing so:

Moving Inward

Just for now
I put aside
all my concerns,
all my worries
about the past,
all my anticipations
for the future.
I put these things aside
for another time,
another place.

For now, I concentrate
on the task at hand,
the task of quieting myself,
of quieting
my thoughts,
my feelings,
my beliefs.

For this little space of time
I wish to go deeper
within myself,
within myself
to that place
where thoughts unknown,
feelings unfelt,
images unseen,
abide in me.

They abide there,
awaiting my coming
to claim them,
to invite them forward,
to invite them
into my presence.

As I move downward,
gently,
gently
downward,
feelings,
thoughts,
memories,
questions,
and images
hidden from me
rise to the surface.

They begin to rise,
and I let them come,
as they will,
when they will,
if they will,
in their own time,
in their own order.

I do not try
to control them.
I do not try
to stop them.

I just let them come;
I let them come
as they will.

As they come,
I do not judge them.
I do not pronounce this one good,
or that one bad,
this one useful
and that one not.
I just let them be
as they are,
and I accept them
as they are.

Since I welcome them so,
my thoughts flow
more freely.
If they spurt out,
I do not hurry
to capture them.
I just record them
as best I can.
As I breathe slowly,
deeply,
rhythmically,
and from the abdomen,
they come more gently.

If they do not come at first,
I simply wait for them.
Gently they come,
and gently
I welcome them.

For now,
I just let them be.
I do not stop them
or attend to them.
I do not worry about them,
whether they are right

or wrong,
good or bad.
I do not worry about
how the words are spelled
or where to put the commas.
Time enough for that later.

I just let my thoughts
and my feelings,
my memories,
and hopes,
and fears,
present themselves to me.
And I record them.

Gently, gently,
images come to me,
thoughts come to me,
feelings come to me,
and I record them,
in the stillness,
in the stillness.

When we have established ourselves in the meditative atmosphere, we are ready to begin the work of the second move, presented in Chapter 2: focusing, jotting, and brainstreaming. To review the flow of the move, then: we write a brief focusing statement, completing the clause: "At the moment I find myself . . . ," adding whatever verb or verbs come to us to complete the sentence. Then we express as freely as we can in whatever form they come whatever bits and pieces of ideas, experiences, relationships, projects, images, or memories we become aware of, without judging, criticizing, analyzing, or censoring them. When our writing comes spontaneously to a close, we make note of how we felt as we were writing.

Excursions and Ruminations

This work of establishing ourselves in a meditative atmosphere is enhanced by a contemplative attitude, recognizing the nature and importance of experiencing, and paying attention to our experience. In essence, this work helps us to live in the present moment and cultivate inner stillness and openness. An Opening Meditation can help us to move into the meditative atmosphere. Let us explore these issues a little further.

Contemplative Attitude

In establishing such an atmosphere of stillness, we help to cultivate within ourselves a contemplative attitude toward life, an attitude that is far more effective in leading us to fullness of life than any method, technique, or strategy. The contemplative attitude acknowledges the delicate interior senses, such as intuition, imagination, and feeling, as much as the external senses of sight, taste, smell, touch, and hearing.

It appreciates the internal and external stillness that helps us to become aware of the more subtle stimuli to both external and internal senses. It cultivates an attitude of openness by which we suspend control of thinking and feeling in order to allow the data of our senses and the data of our consciousness to come to our awareness. Like most human gifts, a contemplative attitude is both a given capacity and an acquired discipline. The capacity is a given; the discipline develops in us bit by bit over time as we nurture and stretch our given capacity.

Experiencing

Our Journal work, like our lives, centers on our experience. Human life begins with paying attention to our experience. It is that first level of consciousness which differentiates human beings from other sentient beings. Human life certainly does not end with experience, of course, or, as T.S. Eliot knew, we will have had the experience but missed the meaning.

Our experience constantly brings us both external and internal data through our two mental functions of sensation and intuition. To be fully alive we must be alert to the experience of both the external and the internal realms.

Through our five external senses we experience what is going on around us, and we gather the data that sets our healing and creative processes in motion. We register that experience through the gradual accumulation of bits and pieces of sight, touch, taste, smell, and hearing.

As human beings, we need to acquire great facility in attending not only to the data of external reality but also to the data of internal reality. We need to pay attention to what is being touched and moved within us as we pay attention to the outer data. Through our internal senses, we gather the bits and pieces of the data of our consciousness, such as thoughts, images, hunches, moods, and feelings of pain and pleasure. This inner data, the data that comes to us from intuition and the other inner senses, is also quite valuable to us.

Our inner experience yields us images and feelings as well as thoughts. Later Journal exercises will draw upon these images and feelings. As we will see, for example, we make our judgments of what is good for us and what is not on the basis of our feelings. So our feelings, too, are part of our inner data, and we need always to make note of our feelings constantly as we do our Journal work. At first, we may need to make a conscious effort to pay attention to our feelings, but with experience in Journal work, we will find ourselves more and more in touch with our feelings and better able to identify and discriminate among them.

Through our intuition, which also has an external and an internal orientation, we gather the data of our experience in wholes, rather than in bits and pieces. In an instant, through our intuitive faculty, we can register a sense of the whole configuration, or *Gestalt*, of an experience.

Attending to our inner experience indicates that we are alive and not dead; we are affected by our environment and responsive to it. The more we see what we see, hear what we hear, taste what we taste, touch what we touch, smell what we smell, and intuit what we intuit, the more alive we are. The more we pay attention to the data of our senses and intuition, the more human we are.

Paying Attention

What does it mean to pay attention? Simone Weil expressed her profound grasp of the nature of attention:

Attention consists of suspending our thought, leaving it detached, empty, and ready to be penetrated by the object; it means holding in our minds, within reach of this thought, but on a lower level and not in contact with it, the diverse knowledge we have acquired which we are forced to make use of. . . . Above all our thought should be empty, waiting, not seeking anything, but ready to receive in its naked truth the object that is to penetrate it. (111-12)

Artists of every persuasion know the fundamental importance of paying attention and often speak of the central quality of an artist as that of observation. The artist sees and hears much that other persons do not ordinarily pay attention to. One cannot truly draw or describe in words a blue spruce, a sparrow, or a Dalmatian, unless one has truly paid attention to particular spruces, sparrows, or Dalmatians. In making an artwork of our life, we must first of all pay attention to the data of our experience.

Living in the Present Moment

Spiritual traditions of both East and West place great emphasis on this kind of attentiveness, or mindfulness. Mindfulness is the discipline of living in the here and now. "Be here now," and "Do what you are doing," says Zen, while Christians speak of the sacrament of the present moment. If we would be one with Life, we must be one with the moment in which we find ourselves: washing the cup, we wash it; sharing the dream, we share it; hearing the sorrow, we hear it.

As we persevere in our patient, honest recording of whatever is touching and moving us at the moment of writing, we will find that bits and pieces of the existential residue of memories will spontaneously present themselves to our awareness. These memories appear because they hold something we need to know in the present or because we are now ready to integrate them more profoundly into our life. Hints, intimations, and images of the future will also make themselves known to us in our daily Journal work because they are the carriers of our future growth. If we are faithful to regular Journal practice, we can expect that whatever we need to know of both the past and the future will be given to us in the present when we need it.

Disciplined use of the daily Journal can help us to grow more alert to present events as we experience them, thus maintaining the fluidity of our lives and gradually and gently integrating our experience into our consciousness, rather than allowing experiences to "pile up" and rigidify.

This is not easy. It requires constant effort and much energy, but its fruits are invaluable. As Jessica Powers wrote, those who live outside the present moment "slide down wastes of time." All we have for growing in is the present, and we best redeem the past by fully living the present which flows out of that past. We best embody our hope in the future by making the most of the present that will become that future. We make the most of life by living in the now of spacetime.

Inner Stillness

While external quiet is helpful for inner work, internal quiet is essential. We gradually become more still in body, psyche, and spirit as we do our Journal work. Each affects the other. Since the body is the *sine qua non* of our present life and the immediate source of our energy, it seems best to begin with physical stillness. This involves relaxing tensions in our body and establishing a regular and deep pattern of breathing. Once we are physically still, then we can attend to letting our psyche and spirit become still.

We can begin to let go of whatever is disturbing us, distracting us, or calling for our attention. We cannot let go of these things by suppressing or repressing them. Trying to do so simply pushes them deeper into our unconscious, and it drains our energy. Nor can we let go of them by deliberate effort because such effort focuses energy upon the distracting material, thus drawing our attention away from the work at hand, the work of letting go.

Paradoxically, we best let go of distractions by focusing our attention, and therefore our energy, inward and allowing whatever material comes to our awareness rise to the surface of our consciousness and float away. What comes from our depths to our conscious awareness when we are still may be significant or insignificant. We must discipline ourselves to acknowledge all the data that seeks to come to our awareness. We cannot, nor need not, judge at this time what is good and what is bad, fruitful and unfruitful, reasonable and unreasonable. Premature judgment is anathema to fullness of life.

Something may come that we need to attend to, but not while we are making these first moves of our Journal work. If it is important, that will become quite clear to us in the fourth and fifth moves of our Journal work. Then we can take that material into the sixth move, decision, with great confidence that we are indeed acting responsibly by addressing issues that are truly real for us.

Physical and psychic stillness prepare the way for spiritual stillness. In the course of our Journal work, we try to relax physically and let depth material rise to the surface as it will, skim it off in our Journal, and remain alert and attentive at a deeper level, the spiritual level, the place that Eliot calls "the still point of the turning world."

To be still in spirit is to be very still indeed. This is the stillness of the psalmist's "Be still and know that I am God." This is the stillness of the external senses that makes way for the internal senses to operate. This is the stillness of deep rest that builds energy for greater activity. This is the stillness in which we can hear the Spirit of Life beckoning us out of our malaise and addictions and dependencies into freedom and fullness of life.

Such stillness is not achieved by an act of the will—"I will be still"—nor by direct effort—"I am concentrating on being still." Such stillness is given. It happens, as we let go control of our thoughts and feelings (acknowledge with equal attention whatever comes to our awareness), and entertain none of these awarenesses (let them all go, by recording them in our Journal). This phase of inner work which lies beyond our will and direct effort and requires us to be open and indifferent also requires great trust that the voice seeking to be heard in the depths of our being is indeed the voice of the Spirit of Life.

Openness

In living life to the full, openness is all. What does it really mean to be open? Being open means first of all being willing to experience everything that is going on around us and within us, as much as possible while it is happening.

Being open does not mean that we are not discriminating about what we allow into the house of our soul. In fact, through such work as the Journal moves, we find ourselves becoming more and more discriminating, more and more particular about what we choose to entertain and what we choose to forego. Being open means that we withhold judgment until all the relevant facts are in. We do not judge what is good for us and what is not nor decide what to encourage and what to ignore until we are responsible for making such judgments and decisions or we need to make them.

Openness is a *sine qua non* of the creative and spiritual life. To bring our lives into focus, to find our way into the future, to be the persons we really are, and to do the things we really need and want to do, we must first of all be open to our own depths because our depths contain the principal resources we need to live authentic, meaningful, and joyful lives.

Much of the time we live superficial lives. We do not venture beyond what is already present to us, already comfortable for us. Thus we deny ourselves that which is not known to us, that which is within us but only in potentiality, that which is present in potentiality but unrealized to the extent that we have not yet been willing, able, or ready to open ourselves to our depths. Through the Journal moves, we open ourselves to the deeper levels of our awareness, recognizing that we safely enter these depths only gradually, gently, and freely.

Opening Meditation

We are drawn into the depths through our own center. To begin to center ourselves, we need to make a transition from whatever we were doing to what we are going to do now. We need to clear out the buffer so that we may be more fully present to the present moment and give ourselves more fully to what it requires of us. To the degree that we are still and open and centered, we can safely and comfortably integrate those bits and pieces that are closest to the nucleus of our true self that arise from our depths.

We do not enter into these depths of our own volition. Still less do we control what emerges from our depths. Rather we prepare ourselves for being drawn into our depths by establishing an atmosphere of quiet within us. For this reason, most moves of the Living

Journal best begin with an Opening Meditation, such as the one above or another we may prefer. The purpose of this meditation is to prepare the way by establishing an atmosphere in which we can begin to center ourselves.

Further, we are trying to be open to feeling the attractions of Life which work within us much like a magnet, pulling us toward our center of gravity, our spirit. The Opening Meditation is only a beginning, only an opening, to that deeper level of experience beyond our conscious awareness.

The word *opening* is used here in several senses. First, we are opening ourselves to our own interiority. We are trying to be open to receive into our awareness whatever in our depths is ready to be evoked. The meditation is designed to help us become more open to letting go control of our thoughts and feelings so that we can be drawn into that deeper-than-objectified consciousness. As both the medieval author of *The Cloud of Unknowing* and C.G. Jung recognized, this letting go is the most difficult aspect of meditation (*Cloud*, p. 70; *Archetypes*, p. 318).

We become open to the sea of molecules in motion within our psyche and spirit. In this sense an Opening Meditation is a start, a beginning to open up to our depths. It is a start in letting go control of our thoughts and feelings and allowing ourselves to be drawn deeper into the atmosphere of depth where we can be present to that which is moving and gathering in us.

The focus of our attention is on being present to what is moving and gathering within us because what is moving and gathering—and ultimately snowballing—in our depths provides the greatest energy and clearest sense of direction for living our true life. This focusing of our attention not only reveals a great deal about where our life is trying to go and the person we are trying to become, but it also generates energy for going toward what has been revealed and becoming that which has been revealed. With such profound insight and energy, we can more freely choose where we will go with our life and who we will become.

Opening Meditation, then, can help us more fully experience ourselves in this present moment, evoke images of what our life is like at this present time, and of what we are like as persons. This experience and our awareness of these images are in themselves of immense value to us. If we also record in our Journal as much as we can of our awareness, we can continue to cultivate, nurture, and evoke those images that can help to heal us and make us more creative in the future.

Through meditation, then, we are able to descend deeper into that vast and profound inner sea of being where memories that still have something to teach us and images that have not yet revealed their meaning and value await our coming to claim them and bring them forward into our awareness so that we can cultivate them, nurture them, and help bring them into being in the world.

They are, after all, part of us and our world. We may be able to protect ourselves from the demons of the deep by living merely on the surface of life, but we may also find ourselves often at the mercy of our unacknowledged demons, and in the bargain, skim over a magnificent buried treasure.

Ordinarily, we must go through many levels of awareness before we are brought to the nucleus of the true self where the Spirit of Life which is Ultimate Mystery is embodied in the unique, specific, concrete, and earthy human being that each of us is called to become. Thus these meditations are intended primarily for persons with little experience of meditation or of writing as a spiritual discipline, or of the combination of meditation and writing as mutually enhancing.

A word of caution needs to be repeated here: As in descending into deep waters, one would do well to be accompanied by a competent guide, and be properly prepared, equipped, and in good shape. Unless a person is quite mature in spiritual matters, it is generally unwise to engage in spiritual disciplines without a competent guide, either an established meditation group, or an experienced individual, such as a spiritual director or counselor. Secondly, if meditation makes us unusually uncomfortable, we might find it helpful to consult a director or counselor before proceeding with it.

An Opening Meditation is a first step toward the inner waters, a move in the direction of answering the invitation "Come and see," a move toward tasting and swimming in the living waters that do not leave us thirsty and that do not toss us aimlessly about, the living waters that flow at our own depths. But we cannot drink of these waters greedily nor can we willy nilly plunge into these depths. Our descent into the depths must be gradual so that our ability to see in the depths can develop.

We have to develop underwater eyes which are different from our above water eyes because we focus on different things. When we see above water we are conditioned in our seeing by what is underwater within us. Our depths create a filter through which we look at the external world, the world of objective reality. We always see objective reality through the filter of our subjective reality, our own under water depths. We peer into the very matrix out of which we peer externally. We focus on what we see there. The purpose of an Opening Meditation is to pull us out of our focus on external reality toward a focus on internal reality. This requires that we relax our control of our perceiving and simply become aware of whatever we are perceiving. The Opening Meditation is designed to help us shift our focus gradually from external objective reality to our internal subjective reality. It does this by helping us to relax control of our thoughts and feelings and just let them come to us freely.

We do not censor our thoughts and feelings, criticize them, or judge them; we just accept them as they are. And we can enter into this atmosphere of depth by preparing ourselves to be drawn into it. We are more likely to be drawn into our depths when we are minds. The Opening Meditation is designed to help us do these things.

Chapter 2

The Second Move:
Focusing, Jotting, and
Brainstreaming

*You shall know the truth, and
the truth will set you free.*
—John 8:32

Once we have established ourselves in an atmosphere of depth
and quiet we are ready to make the second move. This second move
consists of a sequence of writings which flow naturally, one into
another: focusing, jotting and brainstreaming.

Purpose

The purpose of this second move is simply to record what we
find to be touching and moving us at the moment of writing. We
focus our attention on the present moment by recording as simply,
directly, and honestly as possible just how we find ourselves to be
in the present moment. Once we are centered and have made note
of just how things are with us, we gather some of the bits and pieces
of inner and outer data that float to the surface of our awareness:
sounds, smells, tactile awarenesses, intuitions, fears, images, plans,
worries, questions, memories, ideas. We allow ourselves to descend
into our inner depths and scoop up some of the contents of that
flow:

Procedures

We begin our Journal brainstreaming by making note in the
Keyword Margin of the date, time, and place of writing. We establish ourselves in an atmosphere of depth and quiet. When we feel
ready, we focus ourselves in the present moment by completing the
phrase, "At the moment I find myself . . . ," adding whatever verbs

or adjectives come spontaneously to mind to finish that clause. We write this focusing statement in the wider section of the page, opposite the Keyword Margin. For example,

> At the moment I find myself feeling a little doubtful and hesitant about this work. I am afraid of what I might find, yet I am drawn to taking the risk and going for it.

> At the moment I find myself thinking that I do need to take my life in hand and make some hard choices for the future.

> At the moment I find myself wondering just what will happen when X and I finally get together and discuss our situation.

Once we have focused ourselves in the present moment, we continue to jot down whatever we find to be moving in us, in whatever order it comes to us, with whatever brevity or fullness it comes. We may find ourselves recording our anticipation or anxiety about some event before us or recording a dream that we had the night before. Whatever we find to be moving within us we record, in small bits and pieces or big chunks, however it comes, whenever it comes, without judgment, without criticism, without censorship, without analysis.

At some point, we may find our writing streaming out as we explore some issue that concerns us or recall some experience or event that touched strong emotions within us. This is brainstreaming. When we brainstream, we let go conscious control of our thoughts and feelings and just write. Once we get the knack of it, brainstreaming is as simple and easy as turning on the water faucet. We exert effort, but the effort is not that of trying to make something happen but rather the effort of letting go of trying and letting it happen.

We simply write whatever we become aware of that is touching us and moving within us at the moment of writing. We do not try to think about what to write, nor do we try not to think about it. We just write. We do not try to figure out what to write; we simply write. We do not write what we think we should write but what we actually find ourselves feeling, thinking, wondering, and so on. We do not write so much as let our writing flow.

If we have had little experience with journal writing, we may be hesitant and awkward at first and feel that we have nothing to write. If so, we write whatever we can, however little it may be, tapping away at the crust that can form on the surface of our consciousness. Sooner or later, a tap will break through the crust, and we will feel the stream flowing freely.

If we have had considerable experience with journal techniques, our brainstreaming may take many different forms. Perhaps we will find ourselves writing a list of items, a declaration of independence, or a soliloquy. Perhaps we will draw a picture, a graph, a diagram. Perhaps we will dialogue with a parent, a friend, an experience of anger, a project we are working on, or our own body. Or perhaps we will find ourselves writing letters to a favorite author, or wisdom figure, or God. (For discussion of such techniques, see Tristine Rainer, *The New Diary*, Los Angeles: Tarcher, 1978; Ira Progoff, *At a Journal Workshop*, New York: Dialogue House, 1975, and *The Practice of Process Meditation*, New York: Dialogue House, 1981.)

In brainstreaming we let the form of our writing as well as the content be given to us. We write as freely, honestly, straightforwardly, accurately, and boldly as we can, just "telling it like it is." We do not censor whatever we find to be moving in us, nor do we try to force it into a preconceived form. We do not criticize what we are writing, analyze its causes, or judge it to be good or bad, helpful or not. We do not stop the flow to deliberate over correct spelling, punctuation, or grammar.

If we find ourselves stopping to think about what we are writing or trying to control it, we thereby take ourselves out of the flow. We can enter into the depths and start the flow again in several ways. We may repeat the last word we wrote, over and over again, until the flow resumes itself. We may write some such phrase as, "I am stuck, I am stuck" over and over again, and eventually we will trigger the flow. Or we simply write about the fact that we are trying to think about writing instead of flowing.

If we pay close attention, we can actually feel the difference. Flowing is distinct from thinking about, and it feels different. We can feel our inner gears shifting. One difference between thinking about something on paper and letting our writing flow from the depths is that in thinking about something we control the content and direction of our thought. We often need to control our thought, but brainstreaming has a different purpose. We think about what we have written later, if need be.

Here is one journal keeper's brainstreaming on an experience that made this distinction clear:

> I kept wanting to come out of the depths where a synthesis of what I am about was beginning to form, but I didn't quite trust that the depths could handle such a complex problem so I came back to the surface to think it out when I should have stayed in the depths and let it flow itself out, but I caught on to what I was doing very quickly and returned to the depths and let it flow out and it did quite nicely, thank you.

We write at whatever pace is comfortable for us, sufficiently quickly to disengage the tendency to control yet not hurriedly. If we write too slowly, we are more likely to be controlling our thoughts and feelings. Sometimes the writing will gush forth. If so, we do not write at a frenetic pace, fearing that we will not capture it all. We write calmly, at a comfortable pace, trusting that what we need to write will be written.

Sometimes nothing at all will come, and that is all right, too. We do not force or insist but are simply available, trusting that this is not the time for brainstreaming.

At first, we may find it difficult to let the contents of our consciousness and our sense awarenesses flow out so freely and unrestrictedly on to the pages of our Journal. With perseverance and practice, however, it becomes easier. When we are flowing, we know it, if not at the moment then later, when we reflect back on what the experience felt like. While we are learning, however, it can be as frustrating and difficult as turning on a rusty water faucet.

When the flow of writing spontaneously ceases, we make note of how we felt during the flow, unless we have already done so in the course of the flow. Did we feel free and easy, or did we feel we were forcing it? Did we feel angry? sad? happy? peaceful? Were we controlling what we wrote, or was it flowing outside our control? However we felt, we add that to our brainstreaming.

After a period of focusing, jotting, and brainstreaming, we may move directly to the next move of the Journal, keywording with response. If we do not wish to do so, however, or we are interrupted in our work, or time or energy does not permit us to undertake this third move right away, we may do it at another time. But we do not end our brainstreaming abruptly. Just as we moved gradually into brainstreaming by taking a few moments to focus and center ourselves, so, too, we gradually reorient ourselves to the day's activities that await us.

To bring our brainstreaming to closure, we may write a simple closing statement that refocuses us for the activity ahead. Something like, "It is time now to bathe and dress for work," or "Now I need to turn out the light and go to sleep," will just naturally come to us when it is time to stop writing for this session.

Or we may find ourselves writing a "To-Do List" of tasks that await our attention: "Call John. Write to Debbie. Pick up some milk and eggs. Get gas in the car." We let this list also flow freely, trusting that at the appropriate time we will act on those issues and items that we really need to act on and knowing that we may or may not act on many of the items because we do not really need to or we are not able to at this time.

Making the Move

If it is clear how to focus, jot, and brainstream, then we do the work, taking as much time as we have for it. First we focus our attention on the present moment by completing the clause, "At the moment, I find myself. . . ." Then we jot down whatever we are aware of, letting any awareness spin itself out as much or as little as it likes. We continue jotting and brainstreaming until the flow stops spontaneously. Then we add how we felt during the writing and bring our work to an appropriate closure.

Excursions and Ruminations

The writing techniques of focusing, jotting, and brainstreaming engage us in inner processes of self-expression. Self-expression is in tension with dialogue, and both require us to be oriented toward living the truth in love. Let us now explore further these four issues: inner process and writing, self-expression, dialogue, and living the truth in love.

Inner Process and Writing

The psyche is a stream in constant motion, a stream of images, thoughts, feelings, memories, and sensations. Sometimes this stream is frozen on the surface. Jotting helps to break the ice, so to speak, on the surface of the psyche, so that the waters may flow.

Or, it is as if there is a tension on the surface of the psyche analogous to that on the surface of a glass of water. If we tilt the glass, at first the water does not flow. Surface tension causes the water to "heap up" at the edge of the glass and resist flowing. But if we tilt the glass ever so slightly, the pressure breaks the surface tension and the water flows freely. Jotting helps to tip the glass, so to speak, and break the tension on the surface of the psyche and start a flow of writing.

If the flow does not happen, it does not happen, and that is all right, too. We do not force it. We are content with the jottings and move on. It may be that we are really too tired to write, or that we are not really writing from a deeper level. Since there is no spiritual energy or sense of direction in the writing, it runs out of steam. Or it may be that this is a time when we are being invited to rest. Whatever the reason, no matter. We just go with whatever comes to us and if nothing comes, we trust that is all right, too.

This jotting is so simple that it may seem insignificant. As it breaks the tension on the surface of the psyche and skims off whatever material comes, the deeper material can begin to flow more readily to the surface. That is the idea: to allow the waters of the psyche to be mobile, to flow as freely as possible through us without our controlling them or consciously directing them. These free flowing waters refresh and renew us—and they overflow to refresh and renew our environment.

At first, surface material will come: whatever is on our mind and heart at the moment. We let that float off—or we clear the buffer—by making note of it and moving on. Or rather, we let the flow continue moving through us.

Jotting is a form of brainstorming. When we jot down our awarenesses, we are being open to whatever is moving in us and we free ourselves of much of the turmoil within us because we acknowledge it all. Moreover, we have a record of it for further use in our Journal work.

Sometimes, however, we may find that a jotting takes on a life of its own. A mere fragment of an idea or an experience or a question begins to spin itself out, freely and spontaneously. If so, we go with the flow of the movement and record all that comes to us.

This is brainstreaming, a combination of brainstorming and stream of consciousness. Such brainstreaming gives us not only an expanded version of what is moving within us at the moment but also more of the texture and quality of that movement than jotting allows. It gives us not only the bare bones of our response but also something of the riches and texture, the flesh and blood, of our depths (Koontz, *Connecting*).

Once we have recorded what is moving in us, we have it available to us. If it is something we want to remember, we have made note of it. And we need not waste time and energy trying to repress it if it is something we don't want to deal with now. By making note of it we have let it go.

We need not waste time deciding what to write down and what not to write down. We need not waste time and energy evaluating anything. Nor need we risk making premature decisions. Judgment and decision come later in the Journal process. For now, we just write everything down that we are aware of, in whatever form it comes, with whatever fullness or lack of fullness it comes, realizing that we have it recorded and we can return to it later, if need be.

If it is important, we will attend to it in its own time. If it is not important, it will just drop away of itself if we do not attend to it. We just write everything down, trusting that what is good and what is not good will be made clear to us in due time. Repressing requires a great deal of energy, and we want to keep all our energy available for being open to our spontaneous response to the Spirit who speaks to us through our Journal work.

As we allow our thoughts and feelings to flow through our pen, we do not stop to consider grammar, punctuation, spelling. We do not worry about our handwriting. We just write as quickly as is comfortable for us, letting our psyche and spirit stream forth through our pen. We do not stop to think about what we have written or what we are now writing, or what we are going to write. We just write.

To correct our handwriting, grammar, and spelling or to stop and think is to move out of the stream and lose contact with its flow. Such mental operations actually shift us from one part of our brain, the part naturally equipped for jotting and brainstreaming, to another part which is naturally equipped for thinking.

Time enough later to make corrections and think about what we have written, if necessary. For now, we just write freely, as freely as we can. We will soon come to see from our own experience that if we find ourself stopping to think in the course of brainstreaming, we may just as well stop writing. We will not receive the best material that is within us because we have pulled ourselves out of the depth atmosphere where that material is contained. We have shifted gears to another part of our brain or interiority, and it is not the part with the best and most creative ideas.

Obviously, we often need to think about things. For example, if we are writing something for an audience other than ourself, we may need to revise and edit what we have written for a given audience and a given purpose. Revising and editing are very different from freewriting or brainstreaming. They require different cognitive functions; they have different purposes; they engage different parts of our brain. With practice and observation we can readily feel the difference between brainstreaming and revising and editing. Each has its time and place.

Jotting and brainstreaming are modes of generative writing, writing from a deeper-than-objectified area of consciousness, the area where creative ideas originate. When we stop to think about our jottings and brainstreamings, we automatically pull ourself out of the depths back to the surface, thus engaging another part of our mind, another cognitive function, our critical function.

As we attain greater flexibility and facility in Journal work, we can exercise our generative and critical faculties almost simultaneously. We find that we are able to move back and forth between the generative and the critical almost instantly. But if we have overdeveloped our critical thinking functions and allowed our generative functions to remain less developed, we may need to concentrate on developing our generative functions to bring ourselves to balance. If we have learned critical thinking skills and not generative thinking skills, we may need to learn and practice those skills before we have this kind of flexibility.

Part of what we write in the pages of our Living Journal are bits and pieces, fragments of awarenesses of immediate experiences and anxieties, what we often consider to be distractions. By writing these fragments down, we free ourselves of them, at least for the moment. Recording the contents of our inner experience before, during, and after meditation can enhance the meditative experience and provide us with valuable information and resources for living our lives.

If they are important to us, for example, if some awareness of a responsibility that we have forgotten or neglected comes to us, we have made note of it and need not trouble ourselves with it or attend to it now. We can attend to it later, if we need to do so. For now we are free of it, and it need not distract us from going forward with our present inner work.

Or we may have an image of some future project, some idea that is quite attractive to us. We make note of it, a brief jotting. If it is indeed a viable image, an image for something we need or want to do or become, an image that indeed will contribute to our growth, we have it here in our Journal, and we will have ways later to regain access to it and to evoke it further if that seems desirable.

Research into the structure of the brain is enlightening us from a scientific perspective on how the parts of our brains are distinct but interdependent. We know now, for example, that the spatial, visualizing part of our brain needs the word-forming, story-telling part of our brain to make meaning out of its images. Our Journal jotting and brainstreaming provide one way for the parts of our brain to communicate with one another.

Focusing, jotting, and brainstreaming are ways not only to name our reality but to *remain in the process* of so naming. Such naming is an essential first step in the process of recovery from addition. When Ann Schaef recognized that Twelve Step programs deal with addiction as a process, she realized that such programs can aid in making the paradigm shift from an addictive system to a living process system (p. 144-45).

Through combining writing and meditation, then, we are able to open ourselves to a fuller experience of the present moment of our lives, deepening our awareness that our lives unfold out of a present context, a context which consists of relationships and contains, hidden within us, the images and symbols which hold the key to our future growth, development, and transformation.

The key is to be present to what is moving within us and to become aware of what is gathering in us because this gathering provides the forward momentum of our life, the motivating force for our life. When we do not cling to anything but our faith in the Spirit of Life and allow ourselves to be drawn deeper into the flow of our own life, then we can determine to what extent we are ready, willing, and able to cooperate with that flow and more freely choose whether or not we are going to cooperate with it.

Theoretically, we could write without stopping because the flow of life within us never ceases, but weariness and awareness of other desires and responsibilities will pull us out of the flow. To remain overlong in the deep flow of our inner life can be just as destructive as to refuse to advert to that flow. The key is to move with ease in and out of the inner flow as we need to do so, to be able to be in it and also to not be in it.

Self-Expression

As should be clear by now, the techniques of focusing, jotting, and brainstreaming help to cultivate freedom of self expression, a knack for letting go control of our thoughts and feelings and writing whatever we observe to be moving within us. For many reasons, we have simply not recognized how important this free self-expression really is. Rather than stifle or inhibit it, we need to encourage it. Rather than ignore it, we need to find more and more ways to facilitate it. Rather than control it, we need to guide, direct, and channel it. Self-expression is self-unfoldment. It is in the nature of the deep self to express itself by unfolding.

With rare exceptions our educational system has neither encouraged us to do this nor taught us how to do it. Most of us have learned to leap to judgment of the contents of this free flow, or to analyze and censor it, thus inhibiting the flow or cutting it off prematurely.

We must be free to express ourselves in whatever way we feel moved to do so because it is really the Spirit of Life which is Ultimate Mystery that is seeking to be expressed through us. Insofar as we do not truly express our needs and desires and concerns, the world is to that extent diminished. Insofar as we truly express ourselves, to that extent the world is truly enriched.

When self-expression has been either inhibited, distorted, or overdue, we need to be healed, both for our own good and that of society. When self-expression is on a healthy track, it will be creative, however crude, primitive, or imperfect the expression. The principle is to let our inner self flow out as freely as we are able and then completely let go of it, trusting that more will be given later if we really need it, when and how we need it.

In freeing the deepest parts of ourselves, however, we must necessarily stir up material that we have suppressed and repressed. We cannot descend into the depths and bring up the treasures there without going through interior debris and bringing up some of that as well. If we see the debris for what it is—debris—and treat it accordingly, we are not only cleaner than we were before, but we have also gleaned some gold seed-nuggets of creative ideas from the inner stream. Moreover, the energy we have been using to repress and suppress the debris is now free to nurture and cultivate these seed-nuggets.

Dialogue

Much that is not of the Spirit of Life also seeks expression in us. That is why dialogue is so important. Dialogue helps us to sift out that which is of the Spirit of Life and that which is not. Just as important as the principle of freedom of expression, then, is the equal and opposite principle of dialogue. The two together, self-expression and dialogue, constitute a basic dialectic in human growth, development, and transformation.

As each person truly expresses himself or herself it is inevitable that conflicts will occur because one person's need, desire, or concern at one time may not be another's. It is here that the second pole in the dialectic, dialogue, comes into play.

Each unique self-expression is called to be in dialogue with every other unique self-expression because we are not only individuals but also social beings. Life calls us to be in dialogue relationship not only with ourselves but also with other persons, groups of persons, our works, the environment, and our God, however we name God. A dialogue relationship is a relationship at a core to core level, the level where all expressions of being are equal.

In such a dialogue relationship each is free to speak or not to speak; each is free to be spontaneous, without worrying about how the other will take it. Each trusts the other, each listens to the other, each negotiates with the other. There are no conditions, no demands, no resistance. One speaks, the other responds: Word unto word in dialogue.

So we negotiate and mediate our individual self-expressions out of concern for what is good for everyone involved: we live the truth in love. This does not mean either self-abnegation or compromise. It means negotiating whatever needs and desires are in conflict. It may mean withholding, taking turns, accepting tradeoffs, or forgoing immediate satisfaction for something of value.

In mediating through dialogue the rights of all involved are respected, and the dignity of all parties is upheld. Inner dialogue in our Journal can often help us to gain a new perspective on an issue, break through blockages in our inner process, and reveal a clearer sense of direction in all our relationships. As many professional psychotherapists recognize, relationship, at the heart of spirituality, is also a principal factor in the recovery from such addictions as alcohol (Bauer, p. 38).

Living the Truth in Love

Inherent in the human condition is the invitation to live the truth in love, an invitation that we are free to accept to our own and our society's gain or to reject to our loss. Living the truth in love we are created and healed. We are called to live the truth, not only to know the truth. And we are called to live the truth motivated and directed by love.

Insofar as each of us accepts this invitation to fullness of human being, we and all creation have life ever more abundantly. Insofar as each of us refuses this invitation, we bring upon ourselves and all creation ever greater and more profound suffering and crippling; ever greater destruction; meaningless, unnecessary, and premature death.

The Spirit of Life which is Ultimate Mystery expresses itself within each of us as a mysterious and loving process inviting us toward truer and more abundant being. Life initiates, motivates, sustains, and directs us in our life-long response to this invitation to being. We have only to accept the invitation, surrender to the mystery, and let Life itself teach us how to create ourselves and heal ourselves through living the truth in love.

Living the truth in love engages us in processes that constitute what are simultaneously the human predicament and the human solution: the dialectical processes of creativity and healing that require us to be, as Bernard Lonergan discovered, ever more attentive, intelligent, reasonable, responsible, and loving, and less careless, stupid, unreasonable, irresponsible, and unloving (13-20).

Focusing, jotting, and brainstreaming can assist us in becoming more attentive and less careless. Such honesty provides the only firm basis for our intelligence to lead us to reasonable, responsible, and loving action. In this way, through our senses and intuition we gather the data that sets in motion the creative and healing processes within us.

Some of our woundedness can only be healed by the truth. Yet facing the truth of our situation is precisely what we often are unable or unwilling to do. Even to acknowledge that we cannot face the truth is itself a truth and, as such, has healing power. As we may have experienced in the second move, the very act of acknowledging a painful truth can be healing because it releases energy we had been devoting to denial, makes us aware of the destructiveness of denial, and orients us toward a new creation.

As Rollo May (1975) discovered, much to his surprise, women who had been rejected by their mothers and acknowledged the fact rather than repressing it or lying about it seemed to be free of the anxiety that afflicted other women who had experienced maternal rejection but lied about it. These women experienced for themselves the Gospel truth, "You shall know the truth and the truth will set you free."

As we pay attention to one concrete, specific truth that is closest to us in the sixth move, deciding, we make a start at unwinding the complex knot of circumstances and situations that wounds us, holds us in bondage, and prevents us from being creative. As we enter into this process or similar processes again and again, we find the knot being untied, bit by bit, until we reach a point where the rest of the knot dissolves, seemingly of itself, and the tangle disappears.

As Thomas Merton knew, we have only to go with the truth that is closest to us, but we don't know how great that is. To take one small step in the direction of truth is already to be in the truth. Such a small step has a similar significance to that of Neil Armstrong's first step on the surface of the moon: an image from outer space reflecting a truth from inner space: the smallest step that any one of us takes toward truth is a real contribution to the building of a world of peace and happiness for all.

Chapter 3

The Third Move:
Keywording With Response

I have been alive, but I have not been alert.
—Thomas Miradora

Insofar as we have let our writing flow freely in the first move, we have scooped up, so to speak, whatever thoughts, feelings, memories, and images have floated to the surface of our awareness while we were writing, thus clarifying our inner waters to some degree. The extent of our openness and our interior freedom determine the degree of depth of our brainstreaming.

In this third move, keywording with response, we read over all that we have written in our brainstreaming session and pay close attention to two things simultaneously: key words that spontaneously occur to us as we read and whatever new awarenesses are stirred in us.

Purpose

With this move it is as if we throw out our net in a second pass over the inner waters. The net sinks slightly deeper than it did during our brainstreaming and picks up bits and pieces of experience from a deeper level of our inner stream: "the more the waters flow, the clearer they become."

One immediate purpose of this second move is to continue evoking still more data, thus further "objectifying the contents of consciousness" (*Method*, p. 8). This data often comes from a deeper level than the contents of the initial brainstreaming, and it is often more extensive. The keywording can open us still more to what has been stirred in us by our brainstreaming and make us more aware of what is really going on in our life while it is going on.

A second purpose is to discern the categories that flow out of our experience. A growing awareness of the categories of what is moving and gathering within us can refine the interior filter through which we sort out the probably useful and good from the dross and debris that also float in the stream of our consciousness.

Keywording and immediate response also deepen the impression of the material brought to the surface. Since we have paid closer attention to it, we will remember it more readily if we need or want to remember it.

Procedures

Before we begin keywording and recording our response, we prepare our Journal by opening it to the end of our brainstreaming where we write the heading "Keywording Response" and the date in the Keyword Margin. Then we go back to the beginning of our brainstreaming and read it to ourselves, silently or aloud.

As we read, we pay attention simultaneously to two things, keywords and new stirrings. A keyword will usually be a noun or a short phrase, the name of a person we have written about, a feeling, the title of a dream, an issue, a concept, an idea for a project, or a memory of some particular experience. New stirrings are whatever new thoughts, feelings, images, awarenesses, associations or connections are evoked or stimulated as we read and keyword.

When a keyword strikes us, we write it in the Keyword Margin opposite the section of brainstreaming that evoked it. We just write down one or two or whatever number of keywords spontaneously occur to us. We do not try to think up or figure out what an appropriate keyword might be; we just let keywords come to us spontaneously as we read. If several come to us, we write them all down in the Keyword Margin. If none comes, that is all right, too. We just keep on reading and making note of whatever keywords spontaneously arise in our awareness.

In keywording, we are not trying to determine the general category that most logically includes the particular data we have written. Nor are we deliberately thinking about what we have written or limiting ourselves to a single keyword. Like brainstreaming, keywording with response is simply and easily done once we get the hang of it. But if we are not accustomed to it, it may be mechanical and awkward at first.

While we read and keyword, we also pay attention simultaneously to our inner movements. As we find ourselves becoming aware of new thoughts, feelings, memories, or images being stirred in us as we read, we write these new stirrings under the heading, "Keywording Response" which we placed at the end of our brainstreaming. We also make note of what triggered the response so that we can trace the train of initial writing and response, if we later wish to do so.

Here is an example of keywording with response:

...*Realized again this AM how great a distinction there is*	
between process and outcome. I am not upset	*process*
about the outcome in this matter. Quite truly	*outcome*
indifferent. Even glad of...........	
	④

Keywording Response	*process, p. 4*
As I keyworded this, I found myself realizing	
how important it is to determine whether I am	
relating to process or outcome – or.....	
rather the extent to which I am reacting to each.	
	⑥

In recording this response, we follow the same guidelines as in brainstreaming: we do not judge, criticize, censor, filter, or analyze what comes to us. We simply acknowledge whatever is touching us, attracting our attention, or moving within us, as freely, gently, and honestly as we can, no more, no less.

Sometimes we may find ourselves resisting a particular bit of response because we are tired or in a hurry, or we judge it to be insignificant. The response may continue to tug at our attention even after we have moved on in our reading. If so, that is a pretty good indication that we should interrupt our reading and record the response we have been resisting.

At the same time, we need not be compulsive about recording our response nor exhaust ourselves nor spend undue time at our

Journal work. We just do the best we can in the time we have at our disposal to keyword and record response until we have read through our initial brainstreaming.

Making the Move

When we are ready, we go back and read all that we have written during previous sessions of focusing, jotting, and brainstreaming. As we read, we write our keywords in the narrow, right-hand margin of our Journal page. As we read and keyword, we pay attention for anything new that is stirred in us, new thoughts and new feelings, new associations and new questions.

As a general rule, it is best to conclude a brainstreaming session with keywording with response. But we may not wish to respond to our brainstreaming right away, or we may not have time or energy to do so. If so, we leave it for another day. Whenever we are ready, then, we do the work of keywording and responding. If we need or want more explication of what is involved in this third move, we may prefer to first read the excursions and ruminations which follow.

Excursions and Ruminations

This third move, keywording with response, requires the simultaneous exercise of three mental functions and three focuses of attention: reading, keywording, and responding to what we have written. As we do the work of the first three moves of the Living Journal, we become aware of three important processes: questioning, imaging, and remembering. We also experience fear and the need for courage. Let us reflect briefly on these issues.

Reading

Reading, like writing, is a complex human activity. It involves decoding, responding emotionally, comprehending, and judging the value of the particular combination of letters, words, and punctuation marks on the page. When we read our own Journal writing, we not only decode the signs and symbols, we also simultaneously pay attention to the emotions those signs and symbols arouse in us. We pay attention to what they mean to us, and we make judgments of their truth and their value. As we discover the meaning and judge the truth and value of what we have written, we are integrating more profoundly into our consciousness the truth that we have spontaneously expressed.

Keywording

When we keyword, we are really classifying the bits and pieces of our experience that we have collected in our Journal entries. Our educational system seldom teaches us the kind of intuitive classification required here. Ignorance and intellectual arrogance have so led us in the contemporary Western world to overvalue logic and undervalue images and feelings that we often do not value paying attention to the whole range of our inner movements. Since our culture does not value all our inner movements, our educational system rarely teaches us how to attend to them adequately and work with them effectively.

In keywording, we simply jot down in the narrow, right-hand margin whatever words occur to us as we read along in our writings. We trust our intuition, that deeper-than-conscious power of knowing within us, to do the classifying. If more than one keyword for a given section occurs to us, we need not decide among them. We just write them all down. Our keywords are just for ourselves; they need have no meaning or value for anyone else.

Responding

Response: from the Latin *respondere*, "to promise in return." Our response is a sign of our interior vitality and an indicator of our gratitude for what has been given.

Our response unlocks and loosens up more of the material that is clinging to the lower fringes of consciousness and nudges closer to the surface of consciousness one or another of the fragments that have begun to rise to the surface in our brainstreaming. Simply by recording whatever is moving within us, we enable that material to reveal more of its meaning to us.

Sometimes this response confirms the truth of something that had come forward in the brainstreaming, or it gives us a new insight into something and helps us to understand it better. Sometimes we will find ourselves exploring the significance of some item that has appeared in our brainstreaming.

We may also find a chain of questions rising spontaneously within us. If so, we let the questions flow out on the paper without deliberately thinking about them, without deliberately judging them.

We may also find ourselves just naturally expanding or extending a dream or a dream image that we have recorded during the brainstreaming session. Without our trying to figure it out or interpret it, the dream itself unfolds some of its meaning. Since we did the dream the honor of acknowledging its presence, it returns the favor by unfolding more of itself to us.

In responding, we do not center our attention on anything; we just acknowledge everything equally, and in due time those things meant to unfold greater meaning and value in our lives will do so without undue effort or strain on our part. As we pay attention to the contents of our consciousness in this way, we are really beginning to engage in a kind of inner dialogue with disparate, often conflicting, voices within us. This inner dialogue facilitates our acknowledging these inner voices.

That acknowledgement, in turn, paves the way for our eventual acceptance of those voices. Ultimately, keywording with response helps to integrate the data of our experience more quickly, easily, and thoroughly into our consciousness, thus deepening and broadening our awareness, appreciation, and understanding of life and increasing our interior freedom.

Questioning

Another crucial content of our inner processes is questions. As Bernard Lonergan, the philosopher-theologian, has made clear authentic questions flow from reflection on our experience. Our questions are more important than our answers because they reveal and broaden our horizons, the depth and breadth of what we see. As we develop and mature, our questions move us beyond ourselves toward the rest of reality, beyond the personal to the social, and beyond the social toward the transpersonal.

Our growth as human beings is in the direction of deepening our perspective on reality and expanding our horizons. Our growth takes us on a journey ever deeper inward and ever farther outward. We come to see more and to see differently. We ask questions, and one question generates another, or two, or three. We know who we are by the questions we are able and willing to ask. Our questions reveal the meaning and value of our experience. As we ask our questions, we find our way. When we run out of questions, we run out of life.

Questioning is always a risk because questions intend answers. We ask our questions when we are willing and able to ask them. We may need to grow into the answers. Once we articulate a question, we are ready for its answer. Until then, we will not hear the answer. If we are faithful to Journal brainstreaming, keywording, and response, we will find that our questions will become more precise and better focused. We will also find that our questions are like seeds within us. Important questions are planted in us and answers to these questions will spontaneously rise within us at a later time in our Journal work, a time when we are willing, able, and ready to receive the answers.

Imaging

Once we are focused on the present and have elicited our awareness of important relationships in our lives, we allow ourselves to be drawn still deeper into the imagery level that lies below our conscious awareness. This is the level of reverie, a level of being that experienced artists and spiritual adepts readily enter. William James called this fluid and fertile matrix the "fringe of consciousness." Carl Jung, recognizing the profound importance of the unconscious imaging process, developed his theory and techniques of active imagination for evoking and integrating these images into consciousness. Ira Progoff, building on Jung's work, has also developed principles and techniques for cultivating what he calls the "twilight imagery" level.

When we allow ourselves to let go conscious control of our thoughts and feelings, we, too, may find ourselves in this altered state of consciousness between waking and sleeping. We are awake, so we are able to make note of the awarenesses that come to us at this deeper-than-conscious level, but we are not keyed into controlling this flow of images. Rather we are keyed into letting go control of our mental operations in order to let pre-verbal images come forward and make themselves known to us.

These pre-verbal images may include feelings as well as visual and auditory images. Images will appear to us if we invite them, if we welcome them, and if we honor them. In our Journal, we do invite, welcome, and honor our images in the most honoring way possible: by paying attention to them.

We do not try to manufacture images or make them up because images are, by definition, not something we can deliberately manufacture. They are manufactured in our depths, beyond our control, and delivered up for us to acknowledge and accept them, or to ignore or deny them, whichever we choose to do.

When we open ourselves to our flow of images, we open ourselves to the vision of the person we might become and the things we might yet do. In our Journal work, we seek to evoke this vision, to see the image or images that characterize this present time in our life, this person that we now are, so that we can cooperate with the process of bringing our vision to fulfillment. We know that we cannot make images up or force them to reveal themselves to us. We cannot demand that images come or control what they will be like. We can, however, prepare ourselves to receive images. We can enhance our powers of attention so that we will be ready for images to make themselves known to us as they will, when they will, in their own time and in their own way.

These images contain the symbols that in turn contain the two things we need to be creative: energy and a sense of direction. Images charged with feeling and destiny arise out of the seed of possibility within us. Thus they have power to motivate and energize us to realize them and in the process to realize ourselves, to bring our works and our selves, our greatest artwork, into being.

This experience of establishing ourselves more fully in the present is a first attempt to concentrate our attention not only on the surface of our lives, not only on the statement of the surface facts, but also at a deeper level, the level of images.

Remembering

The Spirit of Life lives and moves in us in mysterious and hidden ways. Our past experiences often still contain within them seeds of possibility, seeds which have yet to unfold the fullness of their meaning, value, and joy to us. These experiences have helped to form the filter though which we perceive and respond to present reality as well as the matrix out of which the future grows. Through memory past and present are connected to shape the future.

Many artists find the source of their creative works in memories, especially childhood memories. For example, as Toni Morrison (1984) reveals, memory is her mode of invention, her way of generating creative ideas. Memory enables her to get beneath the distortions and lies of the prevailing culture because she cannot trust such sources as literature and sociology to help her know the truth of her own cultural sources.

Meinrad Craighead (1987), a painter, writer, and mystic, also finds memory crucial to her creative work: "To remember, and to celebrate the memory, is to safeguard the happening from generation to generation. Herein lies the root coherence of art and religion. Both make out of remembering: religion through ritual, art through the imagery that slips spontaneously from the unconscious recesses of personal memories. . . . Like a woman's form and function, the artist is a cavity of ripening imagery, admitting everything to the bed and transforming it" (p. 82).

As we live out the mystery of our lives, we discover that, much like the mystery dramas of the Middle Ages, they reveal the mysteries of salvation history. What is more, they also reveal the mysteries of creation history as they unfold in and through us. As we write out the drama of our lives in our Living Journal, we not only evoke and nurture and cultivate our personal mystery drama. We also tell, if only for ourselves, the mystery story of our lives, the awesome mystery of healing and creating that permeates the lives of those who commit themselves to living the truth in love.

Memory also contains the seeds of our future, still viable seeds, just waiting for the right opportunity within us and within our environment to come forward and take root and grow. We do not know what those seeds are. But we will be made aware of them as we pay attention to the ongoing development of our life's experience. Those seeds that are still important for us, that still have something to say and do for us, will make themselves known to us in the course of our Journal work, if we are faithful to it.

Chapter 4

The Fourth Move:
Indexing With Response

The force that through the green
fuse drives the flower...
—Dylan Thomas

With the first three basic moves of the Journal—establishing the atmosphere; focusing, jotting, and brainstreaming; and keywording with response—we have evoked what is presently moving within us, named and acknowledged its presence, and penetrated still deeper to pull up more material associated with the contents of our brainstreaming or new material previously blocked by debris. By now we have a number of pages of Journal writing with keywords in the outer margin of the pages. Now we copy these keywords into the index at the back of our journal.

Purpose

Most obviously, this index enables us to find anything that we have worked with in our Journal by looking up an appropriate keyword associated with it. The principal use of the index, however, is as an aid to discernment of spirits, making decisions, and integration of consciousness. If a memory, a dream, a problem, a project, or a decision to be made keeps reappearing in our daily Journal work, then we can know with "emerging probability" that recurring issue is a top-shelf item, ready for some action or for greater resolution and integration. Thus the response that accompanies indexing tends to be even more integrative than the response that accompanies keywording. In the fifth move, clustering, we will explore ways to work with such an issue.

Procedures

In this fourth move, indexing with response, we copy into the index of our Journal each keyword that appears in our keyword margin and note the page on which the keyword appears. If a keyword begins with the letter C, for example, we copy the keyword into the index behind the letter C and note the page number where the keyword appears.

As we do this copying, we also add to our Journal whatever response is evoked, just as we did while keywording. To respect the integrity of our inner process and maintain the chronology of our Journal, we simply begin to write these new stirrings wherever we last left off writing in our Journal.

Before we begin to index our keywords and record the response that accompanies indexing, we prepare our Journal by putting the heading "Indexing Response" at the end of our last Journal entry and write the date in the Keyword Margin.

To begin indexing, we go back to the beginning of our keywording and copy each keyword one by one into the index, along with the page on which it occurs, under the appropriate letter of the index at the back of the Journal. If a keyword recurs a second, third, or fourth time, we simply add the page number to the keyword already noted in the index.

As we do this copying of keywords, we pay attention to any new stirrings evoked or stimulated as we index, and we write these new stirrings in our Journal under the heading, "Indexing Response." When we feel touched or moved, we return to wherever we left off writing in our Journal and brainstream whatever is moving within us. For future reference, we make note of the keyword that evoked the response and write it as a heading for our response entry.

As we copy a keyword into the index, we put a checkmark beside it in the keyword margin. If we are interrupted in our indexing or fall behind in it, we will know where we left off in our indexing next time we return to it.

In general, it is best to let some time elapse between keywording and indexing because indexing evokes more response. Theoretically, we could evoke our inner process unceasingly, but not in actuality. There is not only life beyond the Journal; there is no Journal without living. The purpose of Journal work is to help to evoke, cultivate, nurture, and extend our living, not provide an escape from life or a substitute for it.

Secondly, keywording as close as possible to the time of focusing, jotting, and brainstreaming provides an opportunity for immediate response. Indexing at a later time complements this initial response with more remote response which allows what is moving within us to germinate and ripen and sift itself out. Each has its benefits, and each of us must determine an appropriate timing and rhythm for indexing.

Indexing at a later time also provides a distance that is important in judging the truth and value of what has come forward in our brainstreaming. Premature judgment is anathema to creativity. Unless we are unusually detached and well seasoned, when an idea or image first rises to our conscious awareness it may inflate our ego, making us think that the idea or image is more than it is. Or the opposite may occur: we may initially judge as insignificant something that turns out to have real value. Allowing some time to elapse before indexing helps us to resist premature judgment.

In addition, indexing after some time has elapsed also makes it more difficult for us to fool ourselves by cultivating our illusions. It is what we do about the data of our experience, the decisions we make and carry out, that constitute the essence of what we are, the quality of the artwork that is our life: if something keeps coming up and we do not act on it, we call our own sense of responsibility into question.

Until we determine a rhythm and balance best for us, we may find it helpful to focus, jot, brainstream, and keyword daily, or at least several times during the week, then index on Sunday morning, for example, making this integrating work part of our spiritual discipline. If we fall behind in keywording, we may wish to devote an entire daily Journal session just to keywording, if we feel so moved. We just feel our way, sense our time and energy and need and follow our intuition, trusting it, not expecting or demanding to know either whence or whither, just willing to do as we feel led to do and as is reasonable and possible and comfortable for us at the time.

We may find during our indexing that some issue is ripe for resolution. It is a top shelf item that just has to go in the spring clearance sale. We will not need to wait, nor even want to wait, to make this fifth move of clustering. We will already not only know what issue is closest to us, but we will also feel the pressure of our creative energy pushing us to address that issue, to carry it further, to do something about it or with it or for it. If so, we may find it helpful to move on to the sixth move, deciding.

Making the Move

Let us take time now to copy each keyword from the Keyword Margin, along with the page where it appears, into the index. At the same time, we remain alert for any response that is stirred in us as we do so, writing those new stirrings wherever we last left off writing in our Journal.

Excursions and Ruminations

As we proceed with our Journal writing, keywording, responding, and indexing, we begin to realize that our life is not a series of random episodes but that there is some direction, however obscure, at work in our lives. We begin to see this as we begin to see certain keywords repeated in our index. The process of life that reveals this direction over time is an organic process, and it reveals the direction our life is trying to take in bits and pieces which emerge in our writing over time. Let us explore now these two issues, life as organic process and bits and pieces.

Life as Organic Process

To a large extent we are products of our history, but we are also able to transcend much of our history and that is a mystery. Our capacity for self-transcendence is evidence of the Spirit of LIfe which enters into history through nature but also transcends nature and transforms nature in ways and for reasons mysterious to us. However we name them, miracles of grace do happen. Although we are a part of nature and participate in nature, we are not bound by nature. The processes of our becoming and doing are ultimately a mystery, thus they are always more than organic, but nonetheless they are organic.

The continuity of our lives is not linear and mechanical. Our lives do not run on like a machine. They evolve organically. Although our freedom makes our organic growth process different from that in the rest of nature, we can learn a great deal about our own growth and the growth of programs, groups, and institutions by observing the process of growth as it occurs throughout nature.

If we look after the organic, cultivate and trust the organic, the more-than-organic will surely take care of itself. As T.S. Eliot wrote, "For us there is only the trying./The rest is not our business." Facing the Nazi gas chambers, the young Dutch woman, Etty Hillesum, could write, "To worry about the future is to sin against the organic nature of life."

Being organic, our lives unfold in part according to the laws of nature. We experience our lives as unfolding their potentialities, bit by bit, over time. We come to know the direction of our growth as we grow. This growth unfolds over time out of the images for growing genetically encoded within our very protoplasm. As we make our choices for our life within the givens of our natural capacities, our resources, and our opportunities, this growth occurs naturally.

Let us say that we discover that when we are in a time of transition we tend to regress to a pattern that has us seeking security in places where we can no longer really find it, and so we regress. Perhaps we seek someone who has taken the place of our mother or father. We can see that now, as we look back and recall a similar pattern.

But we are not doomed to repeat that pattern. Now we can take a different step. We can realize what we have been doing, perhaps quite unconsciously, and now we can choose to do otherwise. We can choose to develop our independence, to do for ourselves what we would rather have our mother or father do but we cannot have them do because we are too old or they are no longer with us. So we do it for ourself. We become more mature and independent and stronger and able to stand alone. We may need help in doing this; we may need the encouragement and insight of others; but we can do it and we will do it. We will grow up. We will break out of that repetitive pattern. We will go through the cycle again but differently this time.

Perhaps we see that we can go through it differently especially by cultivating a relationship we have neglected, either one we have now and have not fully appreciated, or we see that we need to be open to new relationships. We see that we do indeed need such a relationship. We become aware of that need now. This may be a relationship with another person, a group of persons, with ourselves, with our own body, or with transpersonal reality, our God, however we name and experience our ultimate commitment in life.

Or we may see that we need to do some work, or take part in some activity or project, or we need to get some education, some training that we have left undone, that we once started but did not finish, or that we took so far and then dropped. Or it may be an idea for service that we have had, an idea that we have longed to act upon but have never done anything about.

Or we may see that we need to develop some form of expression, some form of self-expression that we once started, once cultivated, but did not pursue because of the press of other things. Or perhaps it was a desire to learn music or painting or calligraphy or writing or dance or some other art form that we could not afford to do then but we can now. Or perhaps we felt we were not good enough to do it then, but now we know we are.

A model for this organic continuity of our life as it unfolds might be the conical helix. Our lives unfold in cycles that sometimes progress forward and at other times bend back, developing something once left undeveloped and repeating similar patterns from the past. The growth, then, is both progressive and recursive, moving forward and going back to redo, to revise, to deepen, to expand on past experience.

Bits and Pieces

Aristotle said that the one sign of genius was the ability to make metaphors, that is, to make connections and see similarities among seemingly disparate elements. As Teilhard de Chardin saw it, all of creation, including ourselves, is evolving in the direction of complexity-consciousness. The progressive and recursive creative process of evolution is, at core, a process of making connections.

Creative works, if they come at all, usually do not come whole and entire to those of us who are not geniuses. More frequently they come little by little, in bits and pieces that emerge over time. As bits and pieces begin to coalesce and cluster, we can know not with certainty but with "emerging probability" that some new integration is trying to form, that something new is trying to be born.

If this is true, then the task before those who would be creative is clear: we must acknowledge and accept this reality. Then we must learn the best ways to work with it and do that work as best we can. Moves 5 and 6 of the Living Journal can help us to work with the bits and pieces of experience that emerge in our writings.

Chapter 5

The Fifth Move: Clustering

. . . the repository only for ideas which are "moving" and
"gathering" . . . which are "snowballing."
—Thornton Wilder

If we remain faithful to Journal focusing, jotting, brainstreaming, keywording, and indexing, over time we become more and more aware that the contents of our consciousness not only move within us but they also gather and cluster. We find that some of our keywords come up again and again in our Journal work. Often we feel this clustering, even before we see it graphically demonstrated in the index of our Living Journal.

Purpose

The purpose of this fifth move, clustering, is to identify one cluster that we will take forward into the sixth move, decision. Through clustering we come to feel more keenly the pressure of energy of that which is seeking greater resolution within us, and we see more clearly, with "emerging probability," where it is trying to go.

Procedures

To make this move, we turn to the index at the back of our Living Journal. Then we read through each letter of the alphabet, paying attention to two things: 1) we look for the keywords that have the largest number of entries, and 2) we are alert for different keywords that are connected to one another.

For example, as we scan through our index, we may find that we have returned again and again in our brainstreaming to a particular memory, problem, question, truth, or image, and so we see that we have a number of pages listed in our index for the keyword that names that memory, problem, question, truth, or image.

46

The contents of our consciousness are not unrelated or extraneous fragments just flowing down stream. Some particles connect with others into clusters and these clusters, in turn, connect to form even more complex integrations in the five areas of relationship where energy seeks to flow in our lives: relationships 1) with ourselves; 2) with other persons; 3) with our projects, works, and service of others; 4) with the environment; and 5) with God, or the source of ultimate meaning, joy, and concern to which we commit ourselves. A cluster of entries around a keyword indicates that something within one of these five areas of relationship is ripe for action, is seeking greater resolution, or is coming to fuller integration.

The indexing of our keywords not only helps to call our attention to this organizing and ordering process as it is taking place, but it also helps to build energy and accelerate the integration process. If we are alert to our inner movements, we will feel the energy that is building as the bits and pieces of an idea or an issue rise to the surface and begin to gather in our daily Journal work.

In the keywording we become more aware of the bits and pieces, and when we index the keywords we become more aware of which bits and pieces are attracted to one another in clusters. As one person experienced it, indexing seemed to indicate that she had just been going around in circles, repeating herself, yet when she went back and looked she saw that she was really pulling everything together. "It was really snowballing," she discovered. (I am indebted to Georgie Warmack for sharing this insight into her journal work.)

Thornton Wilder's metaphor "snowballing," which came to him in reflection on his own journal work, catches this tendency of the integration process to accelerate. From all appearances, he did not make the metaphor up; it just came to him naturally as he reflected on his journal. As things come together in us, they have the effect of snowballing. We can feel it happening: the snow gathering and packing as the ball rolls along, gathering momentum and picking up more snow, packing in tighter what is already there and increasing in size and volume and speed as it moves along.

Making the Move

When we have done sufficient Journal work as to have a large number of entries in our index, we set aside a space of time when we can scan through our index looking for where clusters are beginning to form.

Excursions and Ruminations

Over time, as we are faithful to our inner work, experience new integrations in our life, and reflect upon them, over and over again, we begin to see where our life is really trying to go and what person we are really trying to become. We begin to see what we ourselves, in dialogue with our situations and circumstances in life, are making of ourselves and our lives. We are given a glimpse of the artwork that is our life, a vision of its beauty, an insight into its meaning, and a taste of its joy. Let us explore now some issues involved in this coming to wholeness: making an artwork of our lives, intensity of encounter, the creativity of desire, and rhythm and balance.

Making an Artwork of our Lives

Our lives are what we make of what is given to us, day by day. Each of us is potentially both poet and poem-in-process. Each of us can be a co-creator with the Spirit of Life which is Ultimate Mystery in the making of an artwork of her or his own life.

The Living Journal is one tool for helping us to cultivate the art and craft of becoming a living artwork, which is to say, a unique and human being. Through the sequence of moves of the Living Journal we engage, again and again, in countless variations of the dialectics of the creative process.

Approaching our life as an artwork-in-progress we can learn much from reflection on our own experience and through the testimony of creative persons working in all media, from mystics and saints, scientists and philosophers, to painters and composers, writers and sculptors. The creative process is a natural, nonrational process which we guide and negotiate rationally. Through this process disparate elements connect to bring something new into being: a new institution; a new idea or a new relationship; a new project or a new painting, song, or dance; or a new human being; or a new way of being human.

As something new is being created, something old is being changed, diminished, or destroyed: "Unless the seed, falling into the ground, die. . . ." We make mistakes, lose our way, and run out of gas. Periodically, we need to rest from our labors. At times, we will need to grieve our "necessary losses." We need to renew our energies and redirect them. Thus, we and our institutions find ourselves constantly in need of healing. With the growing recognition of the deterioration of the environment and the recognition that our society itself is caught in addictive processes, we experience an unprecedented need for healing on a global scale.

When we begin to look at our life as a dynamic artwork and consciously attend to the creative and healing processes in which we participate, life changes dramatically. Instead of merely "living and partly living," we spring to life. Instead of merely going through the motions of living, we really live our life. Instead of merely enduring our life or trying to ignore, drown, drug, or deny it, we really experience life to the full. We engage life, enter into it, and take it in hand.

Instead of merely living in our heads, we live out of an integrated head and heart. Instead of cultivating illusion, we live in reality. Instead of trying to project an "I" that does not exist, we are simply who we are, no more, no less.

By nature, our search is interdisciplinary and transdisciplinary. In plunging into our own creative and healing processes, we find ourselves drawing now upon philosophy, then theology; now upon behavioral psychology and then upon depth psychology. Here we find instruction in literature, and there we find enlightenment in brain research, physics, or chemistry. For example, Plato's philosophical dialogue the *Ion*, the physics of energy fields, and the chemistry of dendrites can heighten our appreciation and understanding of how insight happens.

Making an artwork of our own life and allowing our lives to bear fruit in other projects and areas of service that attract us involve us in a process that is creative in the making and aesthetic in the appreciation of what has been made. The processes of making and appreciating poetry are analogous to the processes of making and appreciating the artwork that is our life.

The words that make up a poem not only refer to something but they also relate to one another, and the relationships among the words, images, and rhythms form the structure of the poem. In a genuine poem, there are no elements that do not fit. All the elements are in such relationship, one to another, that they comprise a wholeness that is equal to, yet greater than, the sum of its parts. These elements must conform to the norms of the language in which the poem is composed.

But the structure is always determined by some principle of organization other than the nature of the elements which it informs, without violating the nature of those elements. What discriminates the poetic is coherence of structure simply as such (LaDriere, 1956). The only principle of poetic structure, therefore, is that of internal coherence and consistency. Thus, the poem exists as a unique wholeness which arises from the elements which are in relationship in the poem and from the principle which informs those elements.

This wholeness exists, first of all, in and of itself. Beauty consists in the relatedness of the elements in the poem simply as such. The poem, therefore, can be contemplated for its beauty in itself, for its own sake. The wholeness that is a poem also communicates a meaning not communicated by any of the elements, the "total natural meaning" of the poem. Thus a poem first of all is; second, a poem is beautiful; third, a poem means something.

As poem, a human being is a structure of relationships, the totality of all the relationships that arise from the interplay of the givens of nature and the environment. In those relationships there are no elements that do not fit. These elements must conform to the norm of the human, but their structure is determined by the spark of the divine that informs, that is, organizes, those elements without violating their nature.

Those elements are in such relationship, one to another, that they comprise a wholeness both equal to and greater than the sum of the elements. As the poem that is our life comes to be, therefore, we will become not only more and more human, not only unique, but also more and more God-like as the givens of our life, under the impetus and the directions of the divine spark within, come together in an unreplicable whole, the poem that is our life and no other. As poem, our life simply is, and is simply. As poem, our life is beautiful, and it can be contemplated for the beauty of its own sake. As poem, our life means something. As poem, our life gives ourselves and others profound joy.

The Creativity of Desire

This most highly creative process by which we make of our lives a living poem involves the union of our spirit and the Spirit of Life which is Ultimate Mystery dwelling within us. Desire is the metaforce in the nucleus of the human spirit, the spark of the divine in us, that enables us to choose to surrender or to resist the invitations of Mystery in our lives. It is the process by which human desire is brought into congruence with Mystery, or Divine Desire.

The creativity of desire is similar to cognitive creativity, which produces new ideas, and to affective creativity, which produces new art objects, such as poems. The creativity of desire produces a new human being, a more mature, more human, more freely giving and loving, unique person.

Most studies of the psychology of creativity distinguish two modes of the creative process, the cognitive and the affective. In the cognitive mode, typical of the creative scientist and philosopher, mental activity is primary and emotional activity is secondary. In the affective mode, typical of the visual artist or composer, emotional activity is primary and mental activity is secondary.

In describing these two modes, authors draw upon examples from the sages and the saints to explain them. Both truth and clarity may be better served by recognizing the creativity of desire as a third and distinct, but not separate, mode of creativity, a mode foundational to the cognitive and the affective and therefore properly anterior to both and superior to them.

The creativity of desire is the mode in which love, the union of desires, subsumes and transforms mental activity and emotional activity into wisdom. An artist of the human does with desire something similar to what the cognitive artist does with concepts and the affective artist with affectivity.

While cognitive creativity produces new ideas and affective creativity produces new works of art, the creativity of desire eventuates in a new human being. Insofar as cognitive and affective creativity flow from the creativity of desire, they produce fruits that build the earth. Insofar as they do not have their source and impetus in the creativity of desire, their fruits diminish and despoil the earth.

Authentic being flows from the creativity of desire and leads to authentic thinking and authentic making. Thus, the fundamental issue for us as human beings is to get in touch with our own heart's deepest desire and live out of that desire wherein we create, in cooperation with the Spirit of Life which is Ultimate Mystery, our own being.

The creativity of desire follows the principle of attraction: Mystery approaches and attracts each human being much as a magnet attracts iron filings. Mystery draws all of creation and human beings to something beyond, something other, than themselves. The energy by which Mystery does so is love.

A magnetic field, one kind of energy field, operates on the principle of attraction. As James Vargiu describes it (1977), as a magnet approaches iron filings its energy field envelops all the filings, creating an energy field around each one. This energy causes some of the filings to overcome friction and begin to move. Thus moving, the energized filings interact with other filings so magnetized and form clusters of filings. These clusters increase the intensity of the field. As the intensity increases, other filings are set in motion, thus accelerating the process in a chain reaction or avalanche effect. At the point where the action of the magnetic field is most intense, the filings suddenly and spontaneously spring into a coherent pattern of maximum simplicity. Acting simultaneously on all the filings, the magnetic field has arranged them all into a pattern which corresponds to the intensity of the pattern in the field itself.

That pattern is the one in which the filings are most intensely magnetized. The energy from the field has flowed to the filings, which in turn use that energy to produce their own smaller magnetic fields. As this final coherent pattern produces the most intense magnetization, it also causes the maximum transfer of energy from the field to the particles.

But what of the nature and qualities of the magnetic field itself? Observation of the patterns produced by the action of the magnetic field reveals several qualities of that field. First, the field generates the most effective, relevant, and simple solution when the action of the creative field is most intense. Second, the magnetic field requires openness, a resistance to premature closure, if it is to produce this pattern of greatest simplicity. Third, the magnetic field is universal, overcoming boundaries toward "ever-growing inclusion, and iden-tification."

As Vargiu recognizes, this activity of a magnetic field's action on iron filings seems to parallel the process of cognitive and affective creativity and can help to explain just what happens at each stage in the creative process. The prevailing common sense view of that process holds that it generally unfolds in stages. In 1926, Wallas postulated four such stages: preparation, incubation, illumination, and verification. Since then, many others have corroborated his analysis or have developed minor variations of it. I would suggest that that process consists of six stages: need, preparation, manipula-tion, incubation, illumination, and evaluation. We go through these stages in progressive and recursive cycles, repeating them over and over again.

Each of these stages is an energy state. A force is exerted trans-forming matter into work. The stages are of varying degrees of duration and intensity. For example, the preparation stage may be very intense and of long duration, while the manipulation stage may be less intense but of longer duration. Within each stage, moreover, there may be multiple mini-processes clustering to produce the final product.

The process is seldom a regular progression from one energy state to another. For example, in the manipulation stage of a com-plex work, the artist may discover the need to complete a minor part of the total work and thus go through the whole process from preparation to evaluation of that minor part before proceeding with the manipulating stage of the major work. Within each stage the force, or energy, comes from both the conscious and the uncon-scious but in varying degrees. For example, in the manipulation stage the energy is almost totally conscious but influenced by the unconscious, while in the incubation stage the energy is almost to-tally unconscious.

In the first stage, the creative process is set in motion by a need that requires satisfaction. The need stage, in general, arises from the unconscious and gradually comes to conscious awareness as the person feels dissatisfied with a situation as it presently exists. As the need becomes conscious, the person feels the need, accepts it as a real need, and desires to fulfill it. This stage is crucial because it opens the way for materials—the iron filings—to be brought into the boundaries of the magnetic field. If the person represses or suppresses the need, the creative process cannot get off the ground. This is why the Twelve Steps begin with the recognition that we are powerless and our lives unmanageable.

Once the need is recognized, accepted, and its satisfaction is desired, the second stage begins: preparation. In this stage, the person analyzes the need, defines it, generates ideas for satisfying it, sorts them out, gathers other materials, data, and information that may be useful. This stage, too, is both conscious and unconscious. Materials are gathered, generated, and analyzed in a free, often random fashion. Consciousness of ways to satisfy the need grows, understanding of the need develops, and confidence in one's ability to satisfy the need increases or decreases. If confidence is not there, the process is probably terminated at this point. If the confidence is sufficient, the process goes on. The function of this stage is to provide the materials—the iron filings—for the magnetic field to act upon.

As persons become prepared to satisfy their need, and confident of their ability to do so, they move into the third stage: manipulation. This stage is analogous to trying to arrange the iron filings with a pair of tweezers. The person arranges all the materials gathered—data, ideas, images, concepts, symbols—in a conscious effort to find a solution to the problem, a pattern that all the materials will fit into in right relationship. She becomes absorbed in the problem of satisfying the need. Conscious effort predominates here, although unconscious processes still affect the manipulation. As Rollo May indicates, the passion of the encounter with the materials in the preparation and manipulation stages determines the adequacy of the final resolution. Desire to satisfy the need and confidence in one's ability to do so continue to motivate this stage.

After a period of conscious attempts to arrive at a satisfactory solution, the person may reach a point of frustration and confusion.

It is like trying to arrange the iron filings in a pattern corresponding to that of the magnetic field without knowing what that pattern is. The degree of frustration and confusion corresponds to the complexity of the need and the quality of the engagement with it. At this stage the conscious mind recognizes its inability to get it together. The efforts are constantly blocked. The stress of this confusion and frustration can increase to anxiety and even despair. The person says, in effect, "I can't do anything with this mess." Desire and confidence evaporate. The materials being manipulated drop into the unconscious. The conscious mind surrenders its autonomy to the unconscious and the materials incubate, cook on the back burners, so to speak, under the autonomy of the unconscious. This is the final stage, the stage of incubation, a most mysterious because completely unconscious stage of the process.

This stage, along with those preceding it, serves three functions: 1) it supplies materials for the magnetic field to act upon—the iron filings, or the bits and pieces; 2) it overcomes friction by setting materials in motion thus making them more responsive to the action of the magnetic field; 3) it clusters some of the materials, thereby increasing the magnetization of the field.

Then, when conscious attention is directed elsewhere, an insight, a resolution, springs to the surface of consciousness in a flash of intuition. This illumination creates the Eureka experience, an experience that is characteristically spontaneous and instantaneous. The pieces—the iron filings—come together simultaneously, as if by a "magic synthesis," into a pattern of great harmony, simplicity, and beauty, that had eluded the efforts of the conscious mind. It is experienced as a sudden release of tension, a rush of joy, an increase of creative energy, and a feeling of certainty that the insight is correct beyond doubt.

Why is this so? When the conscious mind surrenders its control, the magnetic field is free to act on all the materials and simultaneously arranges them into a pattern in harmony with itself. This illumination is experienced as a flash of intuition and a release of tension because all the materials in the unconscious are fused together by the magnetic energy and the force of that fusion sends the pattern bursting into consciousness. It is experienced with joy because of the beauty and harmony of the pattern with the field. It is experienced as a surge of creative energy because the gathering together of highly magnetized materials creates the maximum transfer of energy from the magnetic field to the materials. It is experienced with awe and surprise and a feeling of certainty because the conscious mind, unable to achieve the synthesis, recognizes the power of Mystery, a power superior to its own.

Following this illumination, the insight is critically evaluated, verified, and refined. This final stage of evaluation is largely conscious. It is like rearranging a few of the filings in order to polish the final pattern.

To review the process: a need arises from the unconscious (Stage 1), and it is then considered in a free interplay of both conscious effort and unconscious influences (Stage 2), then, in the manipulation stage (Stage 3), the conscious mind dominates until it reaches the point of surrendering control to the unconscious (Stage 4), which then fuses the materials into a whole. The force of the fusion ejects the insight into the conscious mind (Stage 5), and it is verified and refined by the conscious mind (Stage 6).

In living our lives and making our other artworks, each of us goes through this process again and again, in progressive yet recursive cycles of creating and healing. These cycles may be of varying durations and complexity. Two principal cycles in the making of a human artwork, for example, are the two "halves" of a normal human lifetime, from birth to adulthood, and from adulthood through old age.

In the first half of life, we are born and gradually become conscious of the need to make something of our life, opening the way for the materials to be brought into the boundary of the magnetic field. As we discover and develop our gifts and discover, overcome, and transcend our limitations, we manipulate these materials of our experience in accord with objective reality. In the ideal the adolescent identity crisis with its frustration and confusion brings about a surrender to the exigencies of adulthood and an illumination occurs: a well-integrated ego and persona. During the years of early adulthood the ego thus established is polished and refined.

Then the second half of life begins a similar process. The need to be our whole self, our *true* self, emerges more and more strongly, sending us on a second creative process from need, through preparation, manipulation, and the frustration of the mid-life crisis of identity which brings about the surrender of the autonomy of the ego and persona to the autonomy of the self. Illumination comes with individuation, a well-integrated self, which is experienced as union with God. Old age is then a process of refining and polishing our true self: the consummate artwork that is a human being, a living poem.

Intensity of Encounter

In writing of the creative process as applied to poetry, T.S. Eliot, in "Tradition and the Individual Talent," wrote that the quality of the poem is determined primarily by the intensity of the process of fusion, or connection, rather than the quality of the bits and pieces that are fused (1932).

In his book *The Courage to Create*, Rollo May makes a similar observation. The quality of the fusion is directly proportional to the intensity of the encounter. To the extent that one commits oneself to that encounter, to that extent one activates the deeper levels of awareness. Such an encounter is profoundly creative: "Creativity occurs in an act of encounter and is to be understood with this encounter as its center" (1975). We can expect that the quality of the artwork that is our life will be directly proportional to the intensity of our engagement with the creative and healing processes.

Rhythm and Balance

These inner processes are always seeking a rhythm and balance within us, as in all of nature. If we have gone too far in self-expression, we may find ourselves needing to go equally far in dialogue in order to come to balance. If society has overvalued logic, the pendulum will begin to swing toward intuition. The principle of rhythm and balance holds in all areas of our personal and societal lives.

If we listen to our bodies, they will often tell us when we are out of balance. If we have sat too long, our bodies will get restless and lead us to take a walk. If we have worked too long at a thinking task, we may find ourselves with a headache, our body's way of telling us to ease up on the mental work and try something else for a while.

When we are younger, we can often act out of rhythm and balance but not feel the effects. As we get older, our bodies, weary and burdened by the effects of imbalances long sustained, will give us more insistent messages calling us to a daily rhythm of rest, of physical, mental, and spiritual activity, with time for being alone, as our nature requires, and time for being with others, also according to our nature.

If we are introverted and find ourselves exhausted, it may be that we have not taken enough time to be with ourselves, where our energy and sense of direction are better replenished. On the other hand, if we are primarily extroverted, we may find that being alone too much is not good for us because we replenish our energies and clarify our sense of direction in the company of others more than alone.

If we see only the trees, we may miss the forest. If we have placed too much stress on thinking, then we will need to attend to our feelings. Fidelity to our Journal work can help us not only to discover where we are out of balance but also what we can do to bring our lives back into rhythm and balance.

Chapter 6

The Sixth Move: Deciding

I have set before you life and death, the blessing and the curse.
Choose life, then, that you and your descendants may live.
—Deuteronomy 30:19-20

In the course of our lives, we are constantly being required to make decisions, and we make them more or less consciously. In large measure our decisions determine who we are. Our decisions shape the artwork of our lives.

If we are faithful to our Journal work, we find ourselves becoming more and more aware of the decisions that face us. As items in our index begin to cluster and snowball, we can be reasonably sure that those items are calling for greater resolution and integration in our lives.

Throughout our Journal work we have been concerned with our orientation to living the truth in love, to deepening the atmosphere in which we work, to acquiring the attitudes of openness and stillness, and to following basic principles and techniques of the creative process.

To this point our Journal work has included a balance and rhythm in the use of the techniques of focusing, jotting, brainstreaming, meditation, keywording with response, and indexing with response. Insofar as we have been faithful to this work, we find ourselves becoming more aware of the fact that entries in our index tend to cluster. As we grow more alert and pay closer attention, we begin to see that whatever is moving in us also gathers momentum. Bits and pieces begin to come together. Relationships are formed. Connections are made. As clusters begin to coalesce, they also begin to snowball. They gather energy within us, an energy that pushes a cluster toward greater coherence and greater resolution. As Toni Morrison (1984) discovered in the context of her writing, each piece becomes a part of a whole.

Purpose

We continue with the orientation, atmosphere, attitudes, principles, and techniques of our Journal work, but now we focus them on one issue ripest for resolution so that we may bring that issue to better resolution, integration, and action in our lives. *Better* is defined as more authentic and loving: *authentic,* from the Greek *authentikos,* genuine; from *authentes,* author. Authentic means real, genuine, and original: originating from the author, the origin. Authentic decisions are decisions that are true to who we really are. Loving means truly good and life-giving for all concerned.

As we work with one issue, we will also be increasing our knowledge of our own decision-making process, as well as enhancing our mastery of the art of decision-making.

Procedures

Needless to say, there is no sure-fire formula for making decisions because our decisions are always subject to the Spirit of Life which is Ultimate Mystery. Our decisions will always have, therefore, an element of mystery about them, an increment of mystery beyond our knowledge, our art, and our control. We can rarely, if ever, decide with certainty but only with "tentative certainty," with "emerging probability." Within that context, then, we do the best we can, no more, no less, with the givens of our situation, and for the rest we trust.

Once we have isolated such a cluster in our index, what do we do with it? The basic operating principle is the same as that which governs focusing, jotting, brainstreaming, and keywording with response, the principle of progressive and recursive deepening and broadening. The difference is that what is open-ended in the brainstreaming and keywording with response becomes concentrated in the clustering. We "zero in" on the issue implicit in the cluster not to analyze it or figure it out but rather to continue to evoke it still further through focusing, jotting, brainstreaming, and keywording.

Using the index, we locate all the pages listed under the keyword in the index and remove them. (Sometimes it is helpful to insert a page divider behind the index to hold these pages until we have completed our work with the cluster of entries.) Each of these entries was written on different days, in different contexts, over a period of time. We may be surprised at the differing contexts that gave rise to related entries.

Now we read the entries in our cluster, one by one, in the order in which they were written. As we read, we pay special attention to what is stirred and evoked in us, and we write down these new stirrings, dating the page on which we write. Then we write a brief, focusing statement of just what the issue behind all the entries seems to be. Perhaps it is a recurring problem in a relationship important to us. If so, we state the problem as precisely and concisely as we can. Perhaps it is a dream image that has recurred several times. If so, we describe the image. Perhaps it is a concept, an idea, a truth. If so, we state the heart of the matter.

This sixth move of trying to make better decisions involves three stages: identifying the issue, evoking the issue, and deciding the issue. We remember that we may not go smoothly from one stage to the next. If an issue is complex, it is more likely that we will go through many cycles of identifying the issue and evoking the issue before we have sufficient clarity to decide it and energy to act on our decision. Let us work through these three stages in the move, one by one.

Choosing an Issue

From earlier Living Journal experiences we know that that which presents itself to us first for consideration is not always necessarily the best or most important thing. Sometimes we need to withhold acting on the first issue that comes to hand. Sometimes we need to prime the pump to bring the sweetest, most nourishing, water to the surface.

The same is true with issues for decision. Much of the early work in decision-making lies in determining just what the issues before us really are and choosing those that are ripest for resolution. Even when events require that we make decisions immediately, we may not be sure of the real issue involved. That is the work of this first stage in decision-making, choosing an issue.

Let us say that our work in Move 5, Clustering, has centered our attention on the keyword "discipline," and we may have entries about discipline on pages 3, 5, 8, 9, and 25. We may discover that we have written about a friend, Robert, on pages 7, 15, 23, 42. Many other entries in our index, however, will have only one or two page numbers following them.

As we scanned the index, we were also alert to the possibility that a number of entries scattered throughout our index may all really be related in a way we did not see before. We may discover, for example, that the images of a bicycle, indexed under *B;* a ship, under *S;* walking a tightrope, under *T;* and driving a car, under *C,* are all really related as modes of travel, symbols of the journey of life.

Once we have seen where the entries are clustering, we intuitively choose one cluster that most draws us or attracts us right now, the one that most engages our attention, intrigues us, or feels most pressing. We weigh the clusters in our mind and heart and choose the one with the greatest weight. For example, we realize that the issue of discipline most attracts our attention right now, so we choose it. If we do not feel any strong attraction to one, we choose one intuitively, trusting that we will make a good choice, and if not, we will soon find that out and choose another.

Evoking the Issue

Once we have decided which cluster most calls for our further attention, we go back to our Journal entries and pull out each page on which we have an entry for the keyword we have chosen. The entries arose within the context of the chronology of our life as we did our Journal work. Now we will remove the entries from this chronology and look at them together.

We open our Journal to the page where we last wrote, noting in the Keyword Margin the present date and time. With our Journal open to this page, we read over all our entries, in turn. As we read over each entry, we make note of whatever stirs in us as we read, whatever touches or moves us, those associations, images, memories, or questions that come into our awareness as we read through the entries, one by one, and we jot them down.

After we have completed our jottings, we read them over and draw arrows among those that seem to connect. We follow our intuition here, drawing an arrow between one point that we sense connects with another and so on through all our jottings.

Then we look over our jottings and arrows to sense where the center of gravity or point of convergence of this issue seems to be. Then we state the issue as directly and succinctly as we can. We may find that we have only a vague sense of an issue, just a phrase that conveys a problem or challenge or opportunity. We frame the issue as exactly as we can at this moment, realizing that as we work with this issue, related issues or more precise statements of the issues will become clearer to us in the process of working with what we have. We work our way to greater and greater clarity in the framing of the real issue.

For example, I may see that my entries under "discipline" raise the vague issue that I feel myself to be undisciplined, and I do not like that. The issue may evolve from "discipline," or "the problem of discipline," to "my need for discipline." Or I may state the issue as a question or a series of questions: "How can I be more disciplined?" "Where do I need to be more disciplined?" "What will help me be more disciplined?" "Do I want to be more disciplined?" "Why should I be more disciplined?"

As I allow the questions to flow, I may see more clearly that the issue is really not discipline in general but lack of discipline in a particular area of my life. I may realize that I am quite disciplined about my eating and exercise habits but not at all disciplined about taking care of correspondence. Maybe the questions come, "Why am I so undisciplined about correspondence?" "How can I become more disciplined in correspondence?" "Do I want to be more disciplined?" "Do I need to be more disciplined?" "How can my discipline in exercise carry over to discipline in correspondence?" We allow our questions to flow as they will, in whatever order they come, whatever their degree of precision or lack of it.

The issue that has presented itself to us first may not, in fact, be the real issue, the deeper issue, that we need to address. We will be led to this real, underlying issue, the deeper issue, however, as we evoke the issue we have before us. The presenting issue or question is like the tail of a fish: once we have grasped the tail, we can draw the whole fish out of the water.

Having isolated the one issue in our life that we most want to address right now, we concentrate our attention on that one issue. We do not analyze it but evoke it. We want to draw it forward out of our depths rather than pull it apart.

Evoking an issue requires that we be open to using any of the Journal techniques we have experienced thus far. Or we may find that we want to get a sense of the context or the continuity of the issue, so we will jot down its history. Or we may wish to be present to the issue and evoke images, perhaps using the phrases "This issue is like . . ." Or perhaps the issue evokes a word that we feel drawn to use in meditation. Or we may just want to brainstream on the issue, writing boldly, freely, and honestly whatever is moving in us as we are present to the issue.

In evoking the issue, we do not analyze the problem, the dream image, or the concept, nor do we try to figure it out. Rather we allow our questions to rise within us. We may find ourselves asking such questions as:

Where is this (problem, image, concept) trying to go?

How can I nurture it?

What do I need to do about it?

What do I want to do about it?

What can I do about it?

How do I do it?

When do I do it?

What do I need in order to do it?

Our answers to these questions may raise other questions. If so, we let the questions flow. The principle is to evoke the issue further, recording in the Journal whatever thoughts, feelings, associations, memories, and images come to us, then follow those leads that most attract us as far as we can follow them.

As we go with the process, the process itself will yield us the two things we need to carry the issue to further resolution, integration, or action: energy and a sense of direction. As we go with the truth that is closest to us, as best we can, one step at a time as it is revealed to us, we find that our energy and confidence increase.

When we have completed our work on the issue in the sixth move, we simply refile all our writings wherever they initially appeared chronologically in the Journal. In this way we maintain the integrity of our inner process as it unfolds over time, and we also conserve our resources: some of this material may be useful at another time.

We may wish to spend several Journal sessions evoking the issue by jotting down whatever ideas come to us for doing so and then following up on those that most attract us.

When we have evoked the issue as far as we can, we are ready to move toward a decision on it. Often we will need to act on a decision in order to come to greater clarity.

Deciding the Issue

The deeper we go into making an artwork of our life, the more aware we become of the many currents of movement within us and the many voices often competing within us and around us. In deciding issues we need to distinguish among these movements and voices that are calling us and others to greater life and those that are destructive of ourselves or others or the environment. Ignatius of Loyola discovered for himself how to make better decisions by paying attention to his inner movements. He discovered that he felt differently when he imagined himself doing one thing and when he imagined himself doing another.

Faced with decision, the first voice to be obeyed is the voice of our own heart's deepest desire in regard to the issue before us. Sooner or later, we need to ask and answer as best we can the question, "What do I really want?" Our heart's most profound desire heads toward value rather than mere satisfaction and provides the impetus, orientation, and energy for the organic unfolding of our life. The Spirit of Life which is Ultimate Mystery speaks to us through our heart's deepest desire. Fidelity to our heart's deepest desire constitutes us as authentic human beings (Doran 500).

Frequently, however, we do not know what we really want, and much of our Journal work will be aimed at pulling our heart's deepest desire up to our conscious awareness. Or we may confuse superficial wants and pleasures with our heart's deepest desire. Or we may not sufficiently value our own heart's deepest desire because we—or others—consider it to be selfish or self-centered.

Our purpose in this third move is to evoke a greater awareness of our heart's deepest desire in regard to the issue we have chosen for carrying forward and to determine whether we can do what we really want to do. Then we are in a position to decide the issue responsibly and determine what might be possible next moves in carrying our decision into action.

As usual, we begin by allowing ourselves to relax in body, mind, and spirit, pay attention to our posture and breathing, and focus on the words of the Opening Meditation. As we feel ourselves being drawn into our own depths, we make note of whatever awarenesses are stirred in us: physical awarenesses, the feel of our clothes on our body, the temperature and sounds and smells around us; our inner awarenesses, thoughts and feelings and memories and images. We remain in the depth atmosphere until we are spontaneously pulled out of it, making note of whatever we become aware of, without judgment, without criticism, without analysis.

When we feel ourselves coming back to the surface spontaneously, we do so, gently and slowly. Back on the surface we note how we felt during the meditation and add any detail that we desire.

We read back over what we have written from the beginning of the meditation, making note of whatever keywords come to us and adding whatever else is stirred in us as we read.

This work may well have brought us to sufficient clarity to take action on the issue that has presented itself to us with the greatest energy. Sometimes we need to act in order to gain greater clarity. If so, we act and record the results of our action and our reflection on it in our regular daily Journal work.

But we may also see that the real issue has not yet come to the surface or that this issue raises other issues that need our attention. If so, we continue to evoke the issues in our Journal work, using whatever techniques we now know or will acquire in the future.

For example, we might want to continue to do some jotting. As we reflect on the issue right now, we might want to do some free flow writing. Or maybe there is another person we want to dialogue with in our Journal about this issue. Or maybe the issue involves a group we might want or need to dialogue with. Or maybe the issue has something to do with our body, and we might want to talk to our body about it. Maybe the issue takes us back to evoke memories from our life history. Whatever comes to us we do, following the leads given to us wherever they take us.

As we move forward in action on our decision, we continue to do our Journal work. If we do not see the next step clearly, we do not move unless circumstances or the situation require it. Then we do it as best we can in peace, knowing that the clarity we did not have before will come later as we reflect on the action. Another principle is, once we have decided, we carry through with the decision until convincing evidence arises that calls us in a different direction.

When we have decided the issue as best we can, we go back and keyword, respond, and index the material brought to the surface during the decision-making process. When we have completed our work on an issue, we return the pages we have removed to their place in the chronological order of our Journal. Following the principle of conservation of resources, we realize that this material may have bearing on future issues.

Making the Move

To summarize the flow of this move: first, we determine where our Journal entries have been clustering, and we choose the cluster that most attracts us. Having isolated and read one cluster of entries, we state as succinctly and directly as we can just what the issue within the cluster seems to be. Once we have at least a preliminary notion of the issue before us, we evoke the issue further, using whatever Journal techniques present themselves to us. We address the issue of our heart's deepest desire on the issue. We address the issue of our ability to do what we really want to do. We allow further questions to arise, answering each as best we can. When the questions dry up, we decide the issue.

Let us move into the meditative atmosphere, then, with the Opening Meditation, "Evoking Our Heart's Deepest Desire."

Evoking Our Heart's Deepest Desire

I am here,
in this place,
fully here,
in this place.
I have come apart
from the hustle and bustle
of my life
to take this time,
to accept this time,
to become quiet,
to become quiet
and attend
to the still voice
within me,
the deepest voice
within me,
that voice
that speaks my heart's true desire.

Breathing in
and breathing out,
breathing in
and breathing out,
I feel my body relax,
my eyes,
my neck,
my arms,
my legs,
my whole body becomes still.
I feel my thoughts
becoming still,
all the thoughts
clamoring within my mind
become still,
and my mind becomes quiet.

My body relaxes,
my body rests,

my body is quiet.
I put aside
all my concerns,
all my cares,
my worries,
my fears.
I put aside
my hopes
and dreams
and desires.
I put them all aside
and let my mind rest.
I put everything aside
to enter into
the ground
and depth
of my own being.

I am quiet now,
completely quiet now.
I am resting
in the quiet.

I allow myself
to be drawn
into the depths of myself
where my heart's deepest desire resides,
awaiting my coming,
awaiting my coming
to claim it,
to acknowledge it,
to accept it,
to embrace it,
and to bring it to birth
through action
in the world.

Slowly,
slowly,
I descend
beneath the surface voices,

beneath the hopes and fears,
the worries and dreams,
the dreads and desires.
I am drawn beneath them all,
into my own depths.

And I abide there,
I abide there,
I wait,
I wait there,
to hear the voice
of my heart's desire,
the voice of my heart's desire,
in the stillness,
in the stillness.

Once we are clear about what we really want on the issue, we need also to check our ability to do what we really want to do. "Can I do it?" becomes the next operative question. Do I have access to the necessary resources? Do I have the skill, the knowledge, the contacts, whatever is required to do what I really want to do? Whatever questions occur to us, we make note of them, answer them as best we can, until all relevant questions dry up. Once we have exhausted our questions, we are ready to decide the issue.

Excursions and Ruminations

In making better, more authentic decisions we are brought full circle to the need to know ourselves, to know our nature and how we and others "work." This knowledge centers on a knowledge of human nature in general and our own nature in particular. Becoming and being ourselves require that we move with courage through our fears. Let us look more closely, then, at the structure of our human consciousness, our differences in personality type, and our need for courage as these impinge upon our process of making more authentic decisions.

Self-Knowledge

Spiritual adepts have long recognized the importance of knowing ourselves, both in those aspects of our nature we share with all other human beings and in those aspects of our nature which are unique to us. This self-knowledge is not merely a knowledge of static facts about ourselves, for example, our age or our physical constitution, but more importantly a knowledge of our inner processes, a knowledge of how we work and what "makes us tick," the ways of our selving, so to speak.

Through the application of Journal principles and the series of Journal moves, such as focusing, jotting, brainstreaming, keywording and responding, we gradually come to know ourselves more broadly and deeply because we begin to acquire a habit of paying attention to what is going on around us and within us, and we are constantly processing and integrating that data.

Over time we begin to see consistent patterns in our own behavior. We know when we know something and when we do not, and we know that we know. This kind of knowing marks a leap in our self-knowledge and enables us to make more authentic decisions, that is, decisions truly our own, decisions that flow from a clearer notion of who we really are, what we really want to become, what we really need and want to do with our lives in service of others.

Ultimately, this self-knowledge enables us to be more efficient and effective in our use of resources because we know what we need and do not need, what we want and do not want, and so we waste less and use what we use more wisely. Thus we become more and more responsible for our actions as we get to know better just who we really are and just what we are about.

The Structure of Human Consciousness

As we have seen throughout our Journal work, authentic processes of decision-making draw upon our powers of experiencing, knowing, and loving and move us through higher and higher levels of human consciousness. The more conscious we are of our human powers for experiencing, knowing, and loving that we have been given by virtue of our birth as human beings, and the greater our commitment in engaging these powers, the more authentic and human our decisions and the greater the beauty, truth, goodness, and holiness—the artwork—of our lives.

Throughout our Journal work, more or less consciously, we have been moving back and forth among the five levels of human consciousness that Bernard Lonergan has delineated: experience, understanding, reason, responsibility, and love. As we have experienced, reality invites each of us to engage each of these levels, in turn, yet go beyond each, if we would become truly human.

On the first level of consciousness, we pay attention to our experience. We pay attention to whatever data is coming in through our external senses that pertains to our decision, all that we see, hear, taste, touch, smell: the data of the senses. We also pay attention simultaneously to whatever this data touches and moves within us: the data of our consciousness.

We ask of our experience two questions: What is the external data, or the data of external sense and external intuition? What is the internal data, or the data of our internal senses and internal intuition? On this level, we pay attention, we pay attention to the data of our senses and the data of our consciousness.

As we gather the data of our senses and our consciousness, we find ourselves spontaneously moved to ask questions about the data in order to clarify, understand, and interpret our experience. We ask what the data means, and we use our intelligence to try to understand it as best we can.

As we begin to understand our experience, we find ourselves spontaneously moved to ask the questions "Are my interpretations of the data and my understanding of the experience true?" and we make our judgments about the truth of our understanding. We also make value judgments about our experience as we find ourselves moved to question its importance for us.

As we make such judgments, we find ourselves spontaneously moved to decide on the basis of our judgments of our understanding of our experience. Decision means "to cut off," from the Latin *decidere*. Once we have decided an issue, we have cut off a bit of experience to chew or a piece of a road to follow, leaving other bits and pieces behind, perhaps never to be experienced or to be experienced at another time. We come to closure on an issue and move into action.

Ultimately, we do what we really want and need to do. What we most truly love and desire is what motivates and directs us in our action. Insofar as we are becoming truly human, we will find ourselves more and more motivated to live the truth in love. We live the truth, not merely know the truth. And it is truth we live, not illusion or deception. And we live the truth in love. Faced with decision, in the end we do the most loving thing for all concerned in the decision. The overarching question to be decided then becomes "What is the most loving thing for all concerned?"

The Living Journal, then, is a means to evoke the life within us, day by day, a self-integrating instrument that can help us to pay closer attention to what is really going on within us and around us, more readily clarify our thoughts and feelings about what is going on, make sounder judgments of the truth and value of what is going on, and make decisions that are more lifegiving for all concerned in what is going on. Each of us will do that, however, in our own way, according to our unique personality.

Personality Types

All of us caught up in the mystery and drama of becoming and being truly human in the world find ourselves pulled and drawn through these processes of living the truth in love. Yet each of us engages in these processes in her or his own unique way and timing. The uniqueness of our humanity arises from the particular quality and combination of the givens with which we are blessed at birth and through our experiences of life.

Each of us has differing capacities, more or less fully developed, for paying attention to our experience, understanding it, making reasonable judgments about it, making responsible decisions about it, and doing the most loving thing possible for us at any given moment and in any given situation. Each of us makes decisions differently, and we make them differently at different times and in different circumstances.

C.G. Jung (*Types*, 1971) has given us an analysis of personality types that, like Lonergan's analysis of the levels of consciousness, can help us enter more knowingly and readily into the processes of authentic decision-making. In Jung's analysis each of us is born with a fundamental orientation to reality, introverted or extraverted, and four rational functions, sense and intuition, which enable us to receive data, and thinking and feeling, which enable us to process that data. Understanding, accepting, and working within the possibilities and limitations of our unique personality type can help us to make more authentic decisions.

By nature, each of us differs fundamentally in the degree of our introversion or extraversion. One of our corresponding life's tasks is to develop our weaker orientation to bring our approach to reality into balance. Each of us is born with a basic orientation to reality that is either introverted or extraverted.

As we grow and develop, this orientation can change, but when we are tired or under stress we tend to depend on this basic orientation. By nature and through nurture, we find it easier to take in data and process it either internally or externally, within ourselves if we are introverted and outside ourselves if we are extraverted. Our motivation and energy are also more easily generated either internally or externally, within ourselves if we are introverted and with others if we are extraverted.

In working through the moves of the decision-making process, a general principle is to lead with our strength and check with its corresponding weaker trait. When in doubt, we follow our stronger orientation and functions. Introverts would do well, for example, to attend privately to the data of experience and then check out their perceptions, understandings, and evaluations of their experience with others before reaching a decision. Extraverts might find it more helpful to begin by exploring their perceptions, understanding, and evaluation of their experience with others before working it through alone.

By nature we tend to turn our attention outward to process the data of our experience, or we tend to turn it inward to process that data. So if we look at our habitual tendency since childhood, we can see something of whether we are by nature introverted or extraverted. Do I really need other people to act as a sounding board for my thoughts and feelings before I really know what I think and feel, or do I rather need to look into myself and mull it over alone? The questions are: by temperament which do I tend to do first and which has the stronger pull? Extraverts seem more likely to talk things out with other people, to have to talk in order to find out what they think and feel. Introverts tend to need to get in touch with themselves, to have some solitude and privacy to work things out before they talk to anyone else about it.

But we all develop not only our most natural tendency or orientation to reality. We also develop our opposite, and we need to look to both sources of processing information when we are making a decision of import. Insofar as we are introverted, we look to ourself first, and then we check our perception with others. Insofar as we are extraverted, we may need to talk something out with others before we ourselves know what we think and feel about it.

In making true decisions in love we choose life. We pay attention to that which gives ourselves and others energy and that which drains our energy. We are really looking for the two things needed for creativity, energy and a sense of direction. The introvert best finds her principal source of energy and her principal source of direction by looking within herself and later checking that out with other people. The extravert best finds her principal source of energy and her principal source of direction by looking first outside herself and then checking that out within herself. When the extravert has acted on a decision that requires considerable introverted energy, she will need to spend time with others in order to recharge her batteries. When an introvert has spent time with others in action, she will need rather to have some time of solitude in order to recharge her batteries.

So we have inborn within us tendencies toward introversion and extraversion. To the extent that we know ourselves in this regard, we are at an advantage in making more authentic decisions. To the extent that we are maturing as a human being, we find ourselves bringing these two orientations into balance so that we are equally comfortable operating in either orientation. If we talk prematurely, before we have gotten in touch with ourself, we will probably find it confusing more than helpful to talk to someone about it. And the opposite is true of extraverts. They need to talk it over and then go apart and check with themselves what they really think and feel.

Four mental functions operate with both an introverted and extraverted orientation: sensation, intuition, thinking, and feeling. Through the functions of sensation and intuition we gather the data of our experience, and through the functions of thinking and feeling we process that data. Through nature and nurture, each of us finds it more natural and easier to notice and gather the data that comes through the senses or the data that comes through intuition. Through nature and nurture, each of us also finds it more natural and easier to make judgments about the truth and value of the data by thinking about it or discerning how we feel about it. In both gathering data and judging the data, the same general principle of decision applies: we lead with our strength and follow with our weaker function. When in doubt, we trust our stronger function.

We are able to operate on the first level of human consciousness, that is, pay attention to both our external and internal experience, through our five senses of sight, hearing, touch, taste, and smell and that "sixth sense," intuition. Through our senses we bring in data, piece by piece, bit by bit: we see the individual trees in the forest, the leaves on the trees, the veins in the leaves. Through our intuition we bring in data much more quickly, almost instantly, in wholes, and we are aware of many combinations and uses of the data: we see the entire forest, and we sense the forest's possibilities.

We are able to process the data of our senses and intuition on the next two levels of consciousness, that is, intelligence and reason, through our abilities to think and to feel. We naturally ask the questions, "What do I think about this?" and "How do I feel about this?"

We are aware of what we see, taste, touch, smell, and hear from outside us, and we are also aware of what we see, taste, touch, smell, and hear inside us. To the extent that we are operating out of our introversion, we will be more tuned in to both inner senses and inner intuition, the data of consciousness. To the extent that we are operating out of our extraversion, we will be more aware of the data of the external senses and external intuition.

We do have delicate internal senses that we often overlook when faced with decision. We also have intuitions, hunches, hints, that bring us information in wholes rather than bit by bit as through the senses. Modern culture and education have equipped most of us to pay more attention to external data, the external facts, than to our internal facts, especially our feelings. Secondly, common usage frequently fails to distinguish among feeling as emotions, as affect, and as a rational function. Ignoring our inner data can deprive us of a valuable source of data, our intuitions and feelings in a matter.

Our feelings are the register of our values (Rokeach, 1973). We know what we value and how much we value it by how we feel about it. We know what others value and how much they value it by their feelings.

Exercising our sensate function, we are alert to physical sensations. We see, hear, taste, touch, and smell without judging it, analyzing it, censoring it, or filtering it. In perception our openness consists in resisting the temptation to resist it or rebel against it or argue against it or for it. We just take the data in, as purely and simply as possible. The more we can remain open to the data, the more we will gather. The more we can refrain from resisting the data, the more we will gather. The more we can refrain from judging the data prematurely, the more accurate our data will be, and the less it will be skewed by our biases, prejudices, likes and dislikes, and especially our fears of where the data may take us. The disciplines most operative here are the disciplines of openness, alertness, and paying attention.

And we take in not only external data, the facts of the situation or the circumstances or the event that calls for a decision on our part, but we take in also our internal data. That is, we make note of how we feel about that data, what feelings and movements are stirred in us as we take the data in. For example, does the data I take in make me feel happy, sad, confused, puzzled, afraid, courageous, eager, or what? What am I feeling as I take the data in? This tells me what the data mean to me in particular, its importance and value for me. I need to know this, just as much as I need to know my thoughts, if I am to make a reasonable decision about an issue.

So we take data in from our external and internal senses. But we also need to be alert to our intuitions as we are taking data in. We will see the implications of the data. We will see the possibilities in the data. The data will begin to spin out its possibilities to us. While sensation takes data in bit by bit, particular piece by particular piece, intuition leaps beyond the bits and pieces to grasp the whole picture all at once.

When we find ourselves called to make a decision, we begin with the data: we gather the facts. The data triggers two mental functions which enable us to process the data: thinking and feeling. The facts need to be clarified, understood, and interpreted, thus they naturally give rise to nests of questions. We are naturally led then to determine whether or not our understandings and interpretations are true and how worthwhile, how important, they are. Our thinking function enables us to clarify, understand, and evaluate the truth of a matter, and our feeling function enables us to determine its worth or lack of worth. As a function, feeling is just as reasonable as thinking. It is just as reasonable to make a decision based upon our feelings about an issue as it is to make a decision about our thoughts on the matter.

We can learn a great deal about our own relative strengths and weaknesses simply by reflecting on our own experience in light of the above information. If we wish, we can also take some personality inventory based on Jungian typology, such as the well-known Myers-Briggs Type Inventory and the newer Singer-Loomis Inventory of Personality. (Both the MBTI and the SLIP are published by Consulting Psychologists Press, Inc., 577 College Avenue, Palo Alto, California 94306.)

We will also pay attention to which data-gathering function is strongest in us: introverted sensation, extraverted sensation, introverted intuition, or extraverted intuition? We will take in data from all four, but place greater weight on the data gathered through our most well-developed function. If in doubt, we will trust the data gathered through that function.

When we are clear, or to the degree that we are clear on what we really think about something and how we really feel about it, we are then in a position to make an authentic, sound decision on the matter. We are able to work through our ambivalent feelings, feelings that go in different directions, and our ambiguous thoughts, our mixed thoughts.

As we gather the data and process it, we will again lead with our strength and check ourselves out with our weaker function. For example, if I am a strong feeling type, I will lead with the question, "How do I feel about this?" and check the answer to that question with "What do I think about this? If I am a strong thinking type, I will reverse the order of priority. If a decision must be made and thoughts and feelings are not fully clarified, a strong thinking type would do well to go with her thoughts on the matter, while a strong feeling type would do better to follow her feelings.

Introversion, extraversion, sensation and intuition, and thinking and feeling orient us to truth, providing us with the ability to find data, process it, and gain energy and direction in the pursuit of truth in a decision. We need to lead with our strength and check with the opposite function, using the functions of sensation and intuition in dialogue, and the functions of thinking and feeling in dialogue, while respecting both and depending most on the one that is stronger but checking with the other, the weaker. To the extent that we are clear, that we have no more questions, that the questions have dried up, then we can make the decision. If we need more data or we need more clarity in processing the data, we would do well to wait and continue in our process before we decide. If we have enough relevant data, and we are reasonably clear about it and we need to decide, we should make the decision and act upon it.

We need to pay attention to how we feel when we act in order to learn to distinguish between value and satisfaction. Feelings of pleasure actually feel different from feelings of value. We need to cultivate a taste for value that will enable us to forego momentary satisfactions and pleasures in the service of real value. We need to find ways to have experiences of value so that we can experience for ourselves the more profound joy of value. Such experiences will help to motivate and sustain us in the discipline and sacrifice that value entails. Such experiences will help us to realize that there really is more to life than surface pleasure.

The realization of the emptiness, the hollowness, of mere satisfaction can push us in either of two directions: the search for genuine value and a growing commitment to that search, or the search for greater satisfaction at the cost of value. We run two risks: getting caught up in superficial, often frenetic activity and neglecting our inner work or getting caught up in our inner work to the neglect of our outer responsibilities. We need to be alert to both tendencies, but we will probably be more tempted according to the degree of our introversion and extraversion. The key is discipline and alertness which prevent us from losing our balance in either extreme.

Mere satisfactions do not touch into the nucleus of the true self and cannot fill the void caused by lack of meaning and value. We can move beyond mere satisfaction to value by discovering for ourselves what we really do value, reassessing our values, and stimulating and evoking the deeper values of beauty, goodness, truth, holiness, and love.

Fear and Courage

Sooner or later in Journal work we will experience fear. Fear is a clear indicator that we are being called to grow. The temptation is to deny, drug, or escape from our fear through efforts to control others rather than to move into our fears and through them. In dealing with our fear, however, we need to distinguish between surface fear and deep fear.

Surface fear often strikes us most at our growing tip, the place in us where something new is struggling to come into being. In our Journal work we can allow our fears to make themselves known to us. Then we can assess them. We may not be able to determine their cause, nor need we, in order to grow.

We can consider the direction that acting on our fear will take us. We can ask ourselves the question, where will acting against this fear take me? Do I really want to go there? Where will giving in to this fear take me? Do I really want to go there? Our answers to these questions will reveal our own self-destructive tendencies as well as our growing tip.

Some persons believe that butterflies in the stomach are a sign of fear, but as a student, Robbin Andrews, pointed out to me once, they are really a sign of courage. Courage feels like butterflies in the stomach.

We learn to distinguish these two levels of fear with experience of acting in spite of our fear or allowing our fear to prevent us from taking an action and then reflecting on the extent to which the decision turned out to be good for us and others. We only learn this through taking the risk and reflecting on the consequences because there is no practice room or laboratory for making a trial run.

Surface fear often strikes us most at our growing tip, the place in us where something new is struggling to come into being. In our Journal work we can allow our fears to make themselves known to us. Then we can assess them. We may not be able to determine their cause, nor need we, in order to grow.

Chapter 7

Suggested Next Moves

There is, of course, no formula for living a creative life, no map to follow when we go into the depths. Each of us must find her way alone, yet we do not ever travel alone. People come into our lives all along the way to help us when we need their help and are ready to accept it.

We also have the testimony of those who have made this journey into the wilderness in the writings of the world's sacred scriptures of all religions, the writings of mystics, such as Teresa of Avila's *Interior Castle*, the work of depth psychologists such as C.G. Jung, and in the works of modern creative writers as well, such as William Faulkner's "The Bear." We can learn how to travel our own journey better with the help of these many sources.

Once we have a sense of who we are and how things work in the world and with us, we are in a position to grope in the dark with greater and greater confidence that we are indeed going in the best direction for us, the direction in which the Spirit of Life which is Ultimate Mystery has placed us by virtue of our birth in a particular time and place; to particular parents; in particular circumstances; with our particular genetic inheritance, with its assets and liabilities; our particular circumstances, with their assets and liabilities; and our inhibitions and our opportunities.

Once we are acclimated to Journal work, we will find ourselves gradually paying more attention to our inner movements as we go about the business of our day. This attentiveness helps to develop our intuitive faculty. When we have interiorized the work of the Journal and have had sufficient experience of its value or lack of value in our life, we can then make an intelligent, reasonable, and responsible decision about whether or not we wish to continue using it on a daily basis.

We recognize, too, that once a question, an issue, an image, a "germ" of an idea, to use Henry James's phrase, comes to our conscious awareness, the creative process has been set in motion, and it does not stop when we stop writing in our Journal. On the contrary, that process will deliver up even more to us, often when we least expect it. The most viable hints, hunches, and clues are often given to us when we are not really thinking about the issues that have arisen in our Journal work. We can jot these insights down and add them to our Journal when we are able.

We also become more and more aware of how important breaks are to our Journal work. Although we may appear to be doing little or nothing, a great deal is often being done within us. During a break, when we are resting or engaged in other business, an idea will come, a clue, a hint. If we are alert, we can jot these clues down on a scrap of paper and then add them to our Journal work at a later time.

Once we get into the habit of periodic Journal writing, we will find ourselves "perking up our ears" when we hear something or doing a "double take" when we see something. It is as if an internal voltmeter "kicks in" to register more firmly in our consciousness some intuition that what we have just heard or seen is especially significant for our purposes, or it relates to something we have worked with in our Journal. If we have a project underway, for example, often our best insights into the project will come when we are not consciously working on the project, perhaps while talking to a friend, browsing in a bookstore, or watching a TV show.

We will also discover that the trap door into our interior cellar will open more readily. What has previously been repressed or suppressed will keep pushing up against the trap door until we are ready, willing, and able to open the door. Relevant memories will just arise of themselves as we need them or are ready to deal with them, like our dream images. We try to be alert enough to record these images, however briefly. No need to entertain them or work with them, unless we want to. But as we become better able and more willing to acknowledge, accept, and even embrace what we once repressed for whatever reasons, we free the energy we had been using to keep the trap door closed, making that energy now available to us for creative work.

The Living Journal is a very good place to plan, to center and focus energies and find direction. What is within us is meant to be expressed. Since it is not always possible or desirable to express everything to others, we can express it in writing to ourselves. As we do that, our direction, our needs, and our desires make themselves known to us. We find ourselves developing the images that are within us. We see more clearly what we really know and don't know and what we need to find out. We facilitate things coming together for us, and we can proceed more intelligently along our way.

Excursions and Ruminations

Against the background of the flow of the six basic moves of the Living Journal, let us now explore several other issues that arise in the course of Journal work: context and continuity, relationships, justice, suffering, healing, and compassion.

Context and Continuity

Our lives unfold in a present context that flows out of a past toward a future, not in a rigid linearity but in a fluid circularity, like a "moving circular river" (Dossey 20). To borrow two terms from linguistics, our lives seem to be both synchronic, unfolding *in* and *across* time; and diachronic, unfolding *through* or *over* time. At any given moment, we experience ourselves as a person in a specific stage of a life, but that person we are now *being* is also in process of *becoming*, of growing, changing, developing, and being transformed over time.

As we mature, we realize that the best decisions for our lives are made with a recognition of both the synchronic and the diachronic nature of our lives. Good decisions flow from a grasp of both the present context and the continuity of our lives, which includes images of the future as well as memories of the past. Thus we best begin anything in the present, where we are right now; and we recognize that where we are now in large measure flows out of where we have been and also contains the seeds of a future yet to be realized.

We begin our Living Journal work, then, with the synchronic, trying to open out and deepen and refocus our experience of just where we see our life to be and just the kind of person we see ourselves to be at this moment. We try to be open to a vision of who we really are and what our life is really like at this moment of our history. Whatever we know of ourselves and reveal of ourselves through our behavior in the present moment, however, are but the surface manifestations of a most profound reality: the tip of our being floats like a wave on a vast and profound sea of being.

This profound sea of being contains all those memories of past experiences that we have insufficiently attended to or decided, however consciously or unconsciously, not to pay attention to. Even deeper within the depths of this sea move the patterns of our humanness, the structures that differentiate us from the other kinds of living beings in creation.

When we try to establish ourselves more fully in the present moment of our lives, we are really trying to experience more fully than we normally do the memories and images currently moving within the depths of the sea. When we have more profoundly experienced ourselves as we are in this now moment, this present moment, we are more aware of the present context of our lives. Our greater awareness of the present context places us in a more authentic position for allowing ourselves to be drawn forward into the future.

Relationships

As we mature, we experience ourselves more and more not only as an independent individual but also as an interdependent individual. We come to realize that we do not exist as an isolated individual on this vast and profound sea of being. Rather we exist as a web of relationships intertwined with other webs of relationship.

We find our very selves to be a web of relationships. A bevy of personalities and voices, and a host of needs and desires of body, psyche, and spirit are constantly seeking a harmony and balance within us. As we open ourselves more fully to our experience of the present moment, we find ourselves paying more attention to our body, its needs and its pleasures, its aches and its pains, that which gives it life and that which is destructive of its life. We find that each facet of this "immortal diamond" that we are has its own beauty, each requires its due attention, each enriches our lives, and each seeks to express its needs and desires in an easy rhythm and balance with all the other needs and desires within us.

As human beings, we not only are, but we also make things and do things. We find ourselves to be in relationship not only with our own physical, psychological, and spiritual being but also with the things that we make and do, those projects and activities and artworks in which we invest our time, energy, and resources for our own meaning and joy and in the service of others. Our being expresses itself in making and doing, and making and doing, in turn, help us better to be.

Being, making and doing, we also find ourselves in constant relationship with the natural world of air, water, fire, and earth with its minerals, plants, and animals, all like us trying to live in ecological balance and harmony. We are dependent on all these for our very survival. How aware are we of our relationship with the environment? What aspects of the environment most engage us just now? Interest us? Concern us? We write down whatever ecological issues or awarenesses come to us in the course of our Journal work.

We exist in the natural environment along with other persons, each of whom extends the web of our own being. So we will find ourselves considering our relationships with the important persons in our lives, persons important to us not only because we like them or love them or enjoy being with them and thinking about them but also those who bug us, those who get on our nerves, those persons we find ourselves upset about and worrying about.

 Along with individual persons we are in relationship with many groups of persons, large and small, which further extend the vast web of our relationships. So we find ourselves in our Journal recording the details of our relationships with all the groups of persons that claim our attention. Ethnic groups, for example, our Italian ancestors, or our Polish neighborhood, or our Irish social club. We note our family, our class in school, a church study group, the people in our office or place of employment as a group, the persons who make up our support group for divorced persons, or single parents.

We take note, too, of our relationship with God, however we name or understand God, as we entertain questions about the origins and ends of life, questions of ultimate meaning, value, commitment, and joy. We experience this relationship, not so much thinking about it as being present to it, being present with all our awareness, all our senses, and making note of whatever comes to our consciousness. (For more detail on four of these categories of relationship, see Progoff's *At a Journal Workshop*, pp. 64-85. For a compelling discussion of the importance of the fifth category, our relationship with the natural environment, see the work of Thomas Berry, for example, Chapters 1 and 2 of *Thomas Berry and the New Cosmology*, pp. 5-40.)

Each of these five areas of relationship generates energy for our lives. Through attending to each of them in our Journal work, we can help to free blockages and channel our energy in creative ways.

Justice

When we experience our own life from the perspective of evoking the seed of potentiality within us, we readily see how great a part resources and opportunities play. No matter how great our capacities or our desire to grow, we need resources to nurture that growth. On the physical level, we need food, clothing, shelter, and health care. To become the human beings that we are meant to become, we need much more. For example, we need the opportunity to make our unique contribution to the building of the earth. In the vast scheme of things, no matter how great our contribution, it is but a jot and tittle. Yet the accumulated bits and pieces of human contributions help make the world what it is.

Such reflection casts new light on the nature and importance of the just distribution of resources so that all human beings have equal access to what they need in order to become the persons they are capable of becoming, do the works they are capable of doing, make the contribution to the world that they are capable of making. How often do we allow our ignorance, greed, indifference, laziness, insecurity, need to control, jealousy, and cowardice to deny ourselves or another just access to resources and opportunities that would enable us or them to develop capacities to the fullest? To the extent that we do, we diminish the universe. How often do we allow another's ignorance, greed, indifference, laziness, jealousy, or cowardice stunt our own growth? To the extent that we do, we diminish the world as well.

Suffering

We do not go far with Journal work, as in any substantive pursuit in life, without encountering the mystery of suffering. Suffering is a cry for attention. Whatever form it takes and however it is expressed, suffering calls our attention to a neglected reality, some imbalance or disharmony in our life process. If we do not pay attention, if we do not get the message of our suffering, we have suffered in vain.

Much suffering results from the violent forces of nature, such as tornadoes, earthquakes, and drought. Much suffering also seems to be inherent in the human condition, in the fact that each of us is born and lives in imperfect circumstances, characterized in part by the accumulated residue of ignorance, weakness, and ill will of our ancestors. Acting in our own ignorance, weakness, and ill will we add to that residue and to the pool of suffering in the world. The sins of the parents are handed on to the children.

We find ourselves unable or unwilling to respond appropriately to those invitations for being which lead us to fullness of life. We are not always able or willing to pay sufficient attention to all the data of reality, and we are not always able or willing to act intelligently, reasonably, and responsibly on the data of experience. In short, we are often inattentive and find ourselves doing stupid, unreasonable, and irresponsible things.

The result is suffering, for ourselves, others, and all of creation. All of us are wounded, often without our being conscious of the nature and extent of our woundedness. All of us carry within us unintegrated residue of our ancestors' inauthentic actions, and each of us will pass on to succeeding generations the unintegrated residue of our own inauthentic actions. We carry within us memories of former hurts, rejections, disappointments, failures, deprivations, and malnourishment, both inflicted on us by others and self-inflicted. This residue can cause disturbances in our bodies, our souls, and our spirits which we experience as feelings of anger, hurt, pain, and discomfort: suffering of varying kinds and degrees, from many sources, willing and unwilling, knowing, and unknowing.

Evading, denying, drugging, or drowning these feelings can deaden our ears to the meaning of the suffering, inhibit the necessary cleansing and integration of this existential residue, distort and deflect our creativity, and absorb energy and other resources that might be used creatively. Thus our unhealed wounds and the resulting unintegrated residue affect our present behavior, often in surprising, confusing, and painful ways.

Inevitably, inner work, such as we have been engaged in in *The Living Journal*, brings us face to face with the reality of human suffering. While suffering is ultimately a mystery, how we see it and what we do about it are fundamental to both our healing and our creativity. Healing without creativity is ultimately hollow, and creativity without healing is ultimately destructive.

Thus our journey toward fullness of human living brings us to a more and more profound encounter with the anguish not only of our own particular human condition but also the anguish of the human condition itself, the anguish of the human condition in general. This anguish, in turn, urges us toward a deepening encounter with the reality of God. Out of this encounter springs our deepest meaning and our purest joy. Confronting the mystery of suffering begins with allowing ourselves to experience our need for healing in body, soul, and spirit.

Spiritual disciplines and modern science penetrate more and more profoundly into the mystery of suffering, but they do not solve the mystery, nor is it probable that they will ever do so. The mystery of suffering, like the mystery of creativity, is infinitely beyond human ken. Whether intuitive or analytic, knowledge will not solve the problem of suffering; it may bring us to an ever more profound recognition of the role of Ultimate Mystery in healing. Do what we will, the achievement of healing, like the achievement of creating, lies ultimately beyond us.

Nonetheless, the spiritual traditions of all cultures have always known what modern science is discovering and explaining more and more: that all of us, by virtue of our creation as human beings, have within us powers of healing.

However conscious or unconscious of them we may be, and however consciously or unconsciously we use them, these healing powers are operative within us. Through reflection on our experience we can become more conscious of these powers, and through commitment to life we can evoke them and cooperate with them more intelligently, reasonably, responsibly, and lovingly.

According to Jung, few persons are ever fully born because they fear pain, especially the pain of the mid-life crisis. If we are to be truly healed, we must move into the dread of the human condition, as Kierkegaard discovered. Or, more precisely, we must allow ourselves to be drawn into the dread and through it. Only by moving into the dread and anguish of our human condition can we be truly healed. Like the children in the dramatized story of the bear hunt, we cannot go around the obstacle; we can't go over it; we can't go under it. We must go through suffering if we are to reach the other side: fullness of life.

Healing

It is important in healing not to rush prematurely to being relieved of our symptoms or our hurt, whatever it may be, else we risk not getting its message. If the meaning is important we know that the illness, whether of body, psyche, or spirit, will return.

When we record our experience with meditation in our Living Journal, we add to the benefits of meditation those of writing. As we have seen, jotting down the remnants of experience that arise throughout the process of meditation helps to relieve us of what distracts us from our concentration and frees up energy for the meditation. In addition, we then have access to the depth material that has been loosened and brought to the surface during the meditation. Since this material is recorded chronologically we can also relate it to what is going on on the surface of our lives. Since the unconscious serves not only to complement our conscious life but also to compensate for it, we are more open then to receiving the message within our pain.

As we continue with the next moves that our work suggests to us and with our keywording, indexing, and response, over time the connections which carry the meaning and joy in our life will be revealed to us. As we move into our suffering and allow its messages to unfold to us, healing becomes a creative and learning process, and our Journal becomes a self-integrating instrument and a carrier for the continuity of our life. As George Balanchine said of ballet, "You sweat—and sometimes there is beauty."

Pain and suffering are the shouts of the body, soul, and spirit, cries for attention to what has been neglected and needs attending to, cries for help. In similar fashion, we might recall that when we are not able or willing to hear, body, soul, and spirit may need to keep repeating their cries for attention, hence in our Journal we may find, over time, that repeated messages may eventually get through to us, and we may even learn how to pay better attention to our bodies, our psyches, and our spirits.

Writing after meditation can be most powerful. Through meditation we are brought closer to our center, therefore closer to our possibilities and powers. If we write from this deep atmosphere we are bound to have touched into our deeper self and that is why it is a doorway to our destiny, a doorway to our healing and creating ourselves. Writing helps to release the distractions that hold us back. This combination of meditation and writing combines being and becoming, doing and appreciating.

Life moves forward through ever recurrent cycles of creating and healing. As the story of creation is told in the Old Testament, God worked for six days to create the world and rested on the seventh. Following this pattern, our Western culture traditionally has recognized that human beings need a Sabbath, or day of rest, for every six of work. In similar fashion, the creative work of the day tires us, and we need sleep to recover our energies. In the seasons of the year there is the work of planting, cultivating, and harvesting in the seasons of spring, summer, and autumn and then the resting during the winter months. All of nature speaks of this reality that when anything creative comes into being, something else is destroyed, lost, or left behind, something must be repaired, recovered, replaced, or mourned. When the chicken comes out of the egg, the shell is destroyed, and the chick must adjust to a new environment before being able to go out and really be a chicken. The realization of a new idea means the leaving behind of an old or a change in the old. The creation of a new person means the shedding of old ways, the loss of old and comfortable habits.

All around us we see that creation always involves in some way a loss, a wound, and in our trying to live creative lives we find ourselves wounded often by misunderstanding, rejection, disappointment, and failure. Our bodies, too, reflect this reality. They are subject to invasion and harm both from without and within ourselves. Our psyches and our spirits, too, are subject to wounding. So we need to be healed, all of us, throughout the course of our lives.

Healing partakes of degrees. At its most superficial level, healing is the relief or control of pain. The deeper levels of healing, however, increase our capacities for freedom, meaning, and joy in life. When we open ourselves to experiencing whatever suffering is truly ours to bear, we create a fertile ground for that suffering to shed its deepest and most precious meaning. We find ourselves growing in a more profound wisdom and a steadier commitment to enriching and enhancing life. This wisdom and commitment enable us to take some action to correct the imbalance and disharmony that the suffering was calling our attention to. Or it enables us to accept and transcend whatever suffering cannot be removed.

Spiritual traditions of both East and West have long known methods of evoking our inner powers of healing. Modern science develops its capacity to describe what happens physiologically in healing and to explain in some measure what occurs. Nonetheless, in healing as in suffering, an element of Mystery, an increment of reality beyond our control and beyond our explanation, always remains. While there are great possibilities for healing within us, there are also limits, possibilities and limits of genetic inheritance as well as those accrued through living. External reality, too, imposes its limits and opens up possibilities for healing. As a race and as individuals we do not know either our limitations or our possibilities for healing. We come to know these only through living—and reflecting on our experience.

Compassion

As Ibsen's play *The Wild Duck* so powerfully dramatizes, truth pursued through any other motive than compassion can be destructive. Love, particularly in the form of compassion for ourselves, provides the energy and commitment to be open to truth and prevents it from crushing us. Human survival requires that we live the truth—not just talk about truth or think about truth—and that we live it in love.

Compassion is that expression of love that enables us to be in genuine solidarity with the suffering one, whether that one be ourselves or another. Compassion enables us to be in relationship with a sufferer not as master or superior, but simply as another being, a being in pain, a being in need of healing. It is the capacity to feel *with*, to suffer *with*, another.

Compassion for people in their suffering was what motivated Jesus of Nazareth. As the Christian Gospels eloquently demonstrate, Jesus was moved with compassion for the suffering of others. Being *with* those who suffered, he was able to evoke the power of faith that lay dormant in them, and they found themselves healed.

Conclusion

Nature never sleeps. The process of life never stands still. The creation has not come to an end. The Bible says that God created [humans] on the sixth day and rested . . . . That day of rest must have been the beginning of the second week. We are children of the eighth day.
—Thornton Wilder, *The Eighth Day*

Until we have had some experience with journal writing, we may confuse a journal with a diary. This confusion can inhibit effective use of a journal. With experience, however, we can not only understand the differences between the two more clearly but also actually feel those differences as well.

A journal usually penetrates deeper than a diary and extends far beyond it. While a diary is primarily a chronological record of past events, a journal goes beyond recording facts and events to evoking the meaning and value of those events. Like a diary, a journal is empirically based and, as such, is rooted in facts. The facts that find their way into our journals, however, are not fixed and inert objects but bits and pieces of the "pulsing flow" of our life. As Thornton Wilder discovered much to his puzzlement, there was nothing static in his journals, but only that which was moving, gathering, and snowballing within him. (See *The Journals of Thornton Wilder* (1939-1961), D. Gallup, ed. Yale University Press, 1985.)

Since the development of writing, creative persons in numerous places and walks of life have written personal journals in which they evoked and nurtured their lives and their works. Reflections on the *how* of their journal work, however, when they occur at all, are usually sporadic and unsystematic: it is one thing to do, another to reflect on what one is doing, still another to reflect accurately, and yet another to communicate effectively what one is doing.

Like life itself, this book is necessarily tentative and eclectic, drawing what it can from specialized disciplines of study while forging ahead into a land of no-field and all-fields which comprehends all disciplines yet transcends them all. Like life itself, it draws upon some of the best of scholars as well as upon some of those who make no claim to scholarship but learn from Life and share what they learn: "from hand to hand the bread of life is passed." The principal criterion for evaluating all these sources is reliability; the principal criterion for evaluating reliability is truth to experience.

Faith and Belief

Our acceptance of Life's invitation to being does not require that we profess any particular system of beliefs; it does require that we possess a profound faith in the Spirit of Life which is Ultimate Mystery.

The creative and healing processes spring from a depth within us beneath all words and therefore necessarily beneath all religious, philosophical, sociological, and psychological beliefs. These processes also stretch toward a reality infinitely beyond us. We cannot figure them out with our heads; we can only live them out with our whole being. Insofar as we come to understand them at all, we do so in the living, not merely in the thinking. To our joy, we cooperate with these processes as given; to our peril, we refuse to cooperate with these processes as given.

Again and again, reflection on the whence, the why, and the how of these processes finds itself confronting the problems of faith, belief, and language which turn upon our understanding of the nature of reality, especially our own human reality. In Robert Doran's analysis, we are composed of "spirit and matter, to be joined by negotiating the psyche, which shares in both" (861). In Thomas Berry's words, we are beings "in whom the universe reflects on and celebrates itself in conscious self-awareness" (18).

We are enabled to create and unify ourselves and reflect upon the universe and celebrate it through a deep structure, a medial structure, and a surface structure. Faith from the deep structure animates the surface structure through the medial structure; the medial structure channels faith from the deep structure to the surface structure where it is expressed in behavior, including words. Faith emanates from the deep structure while beliefs originate in the medial structure. Beliefs are uttered while faith is beyond words.

Our beliefs are important because they enable us to articulate something of our faith and thus integrate our faith more profoundly into our personalities. As Ira Progoff expresses the heart of the matter: "We must remain within the terms of our doctrines, whatever they be, for they provide the symbols that can unfold for us from the particular to the universal. At the same time we must remain open to the spontaneity of events so that they can expand our perceptions within the framework of our doctrines" (*Process Meditation*, 234).

"What is your faith" is a far more profound question than "What is your belief?" Faith is fundamental to human life. For example, the cabbage seed need not have faith in the Spirit of Life to become a cabbage. The egg of the blue jay need not have such faith to become a blue jay nor the Dalmatian embryo to become a Dalmatian. If you and I are to transcend the level of being of cabbage, blue jay, and Dalmatian and become fully human, however, we must grow in faith in the Spirit of Life.

Life is the crucible of faith. Life constantly and indiscriminately offers faith in the Spirit of Life to each of us. This faith, however, is mediated through the unique personality, cultures, and circumstances in which we are born. At different times and to varying degrees, our personality, cultures, and circumstances weaken, distort, or destroy our faith in Life, or they strengthen, clarify, and build that faith. While beliefs come and go, our experience of life constantly reveals and tests our faith.

We express our vision of reality through our beliefs, but we live or die according to the faith that animates that vision. We either live our faith in the Spirit of Life, or we do not, and our lives will reveal our faith or lack of it. To the extent that faith animates us, we live a human life. To the extent that such a faith does not animate us, we do not come into existence as a human being.

Normal human growth, development, and transformation require a resolute and deepening faith and a radical openness to the critique, change, and development of our beliefs. This is why the greatest challenge before us today is the problem of faith and belief. This is why we must do all that we can to allow and enable ourselves and others to be drawn beneath the surface and medial structures of life to the deep structure. This is why we must become better able and more willing to evoke the lifegiving spirit beneath destructive behaviors. This is why we must respect beliefs about reality different from our own yet transcend them to cultivate and nurture a strong, perduring faith in the Spirit of Life which is Ultimate Mystery.

Dietrich Bonhoeffer raised the question, "How can we speak of God in a world come of age?" That question still poses a profound challenge for anyone who would communicate about realities that touch into the depths of human experience. We should not be discouraged, therefore, if we find it difficult to express ourselves in a language potentially accessible to all human beings, whatever their beliefs about Life. If we need a transcultural symbol system, we must wait patiently for it to emerge out of our shared experience of life. In the meantime, we should not be surprised if we are sometimes misunderstood as we do the best we can, to communicate our faith and our beliefs.

I am a woman born in America to a Catholic family and a member of the religious congregation of the Sisters of Mercy. My formal education in public elementary and high schools and Catholic universities is complemented by self-education through living, reflecting, and a range of reading in other traditions and other cultures. In writing this book, I have continued to struggle for an authentic language that will allow me to speak honestly out of my faith in a free and loving God Who is manifested to us as the Spirit of Life which is Ultimate Mystery and remain true to my own religious beliefs while also speaking effectively to the hearts and minds of persons who may share my faith yet not share my Catholic Christian beliefs.

We cannot but be what we are, and that is what we have allowed Life to make of us within the context of our personality, cultures, and circumstances. What we are and what we do speak our faith far more dramatically and eloquently than any expression in words. If we dare to allow our deep structure to reveal itself to others in words, however, we cannot speak or write authentically but out of our own experience and through the acquired symbol system of our languages, while taking into account our own bias and hardness of heart.

By the same token, others can only be what they are and understand us or fail to understand us out of their experience and through the terms of their language. If we dare to express ourselves, we must also take care to do so in ways that will make it possible for our audience to understand us, while keeping in mind that their biases and hardness of heart may distort their understanding.

In self-expression, then, we must do the best we can, to be authentic. In communication, we do the best we can, to be effective. Union of authentic expression and effective communication is the ideal.

Living our faith in the Spirit of Life, like all journeys into deep waters and beyond the frontiers of space, is always a risk. It is a journey ever deeper into the nucleus of our true self and ever outward toward other human beings, the rest of creation, and Ultimate Mystery. We simply do not know all that lies within our depths or beyond our present horizons, nor can we know except as we live out our lives rooted in our own depths and stretching toward new horizons.

Truth and the freedom to live the truth in love are matters of commitment and fidelity. They are offered to us freely, and they are priceless. At the same time, we do not accept them readily. They do not come easy, nor are they cheap. If we want them, we must be prepared to pay the price. In plumbing our own depths and expanding our horizons, we can expect to let go of our illusions, one by one. Sometimes, if we have been inattentive or particularly resistant to reality, we may find our illusions being peeled off or even torn away from us. If we are gentle with ourselves, however, we will shed them softly because we no longer need them.

When we live out of our depths, we stop trying to change anyone, including ourselves. Rather we allow life to change and transform us, thus setting up a chain reaction that builds greater and greater energy and sets a clearer and clearer direction. Such a chain reaction of organic change shows promise, even in this Age of Destruction, of one day reaching such an intensity that a critical mass of children of the eighth day will accomplish the quantum leap into a new Age of Creation, a whole new way of human being.

We begin the process of decision-making in faith in Life which is Ultimate Mystery, a faith that tells us that life is ultimately beneficent and we can trust the processes of life to be about our making and not our undoing, if we attend to those processes attentively, intelligently, reasonably, responsibly, and lovingly. In the end, we are brought back to faith in the Spirit of Life because we simply do not know what decisions are truly good and which ones ultimately are not truly good. We do the best we can with what we have been given and then remain in peace, trusting in Life.

Just as the origin of things is infinitely beyond our knowing or controlling, so, too, are the ultimate ends of things beyond our knowledge or control. What matters is that we come to trust Life more and more as we act and reflect on our actions, that we also come to trust ourselves more and more as we act and reflect on our actions.

As we make decisions, savor the effects and reflect on them, we build the foundations of the persons we are. We make the artwork that is our life. Out of this foundation, this grounding, we are in a better position to determine the principles by which we live and organize them into a coherent system. This system of principles then conditions and motivates and directs our further decisions as we go again through the progressive and recursive processes of creating and healing that bring about new works and make of us a new person.

From this perspective, faith can be defined as the belief that "anything is possible, anything can be." Faith is an almighty power that can transcend limitations and attain the seemingly impossible. It is a profound conviction that something good can and will happen and a commitment to do whatever is necessary to bring that good about. Faith is the opposite of fatalism or hopeless resignation to what is. If we are in need of healing, faith believes that we can be healed, that we can know what to do and what not to do to bring about our healing, and that we can do what is good for us and cease doing what is not good for us to bring about our healing. Faith is surrender to Mystery, surrender to the ultimate source and the ultimate outcome of all of creation.

Mystery has implanted a major source of our creating and healing within us. Genetically encoded in us as human beings is this source that we seek to activate when we seek to evoke our powers of inner healing and creating. The limits and possibilities of this source are infinitely beyond our knowing beforehand, and in faith we surrender to those limits and possibilities. We do what we can, to open ourselves to creating and healing, being created and healed, and then we are at peace, whatever the outcome.

Modern scientists are discovering and investigating the power of faith to heal. For example, Herbert Benson, a medical doctor teaching at Harvard, in his most recent book explores the workings of faith in healing. His research in the United States and the Himalayas has led him to say that the powers of persons with profound beliefs are difficult to limit. Like other scientists and medical doctors, trying to bridge the two disciplines of faith and science, Benson and other scientists are discovering that profound beliefs, whatever their focus, can play a significant part in generating healing responses in the body.

Every religious tradition has been blessed with persons who seemed to have access to unusual powers of healing, faith healers, shamans, medicine women, who invoke their own healing powers along with herbs and medicines often in the service of healing another. The New Testament contains stories of how Jesus of Nazareth healed lepers, persons possessed by evil spirits and all manner of ailments, even raising Lazarus from the dead. His miracles attracted many followers to him, many seeking His healing powers. But as Albert Nolan points out, Jesus made it quite clear that *he* did not heal. Rather, healing occurred by the person's *faith*. Again and again the Gospel writers tell us that faith is what heals. Faith is also what creates us and our world.

Commitment

A great need today is for persons who commit themselves to resist self-destructive tendencies, both as individuals and as a society. All of us, to greater or lesser degree, have self-destructive as well as self-constructive tendencies. As we grow, we are constantly being asked to make choices as to whether we will grow or not, whether we will continue works and relationships and situations that are destructive or constructive of our growth. When we have a sense of what is good for us and what is not and what is good for others and what is not—good defined as what contributes to growth toward maturity and fulfillment of the potential within the seed—we can make more conscious choices, therefore become more responsible for our own growth and the growth of our world.

Self-fulfillment then is seen not in a superficial sense of feeling good but rather in a root sense of truly fulfilling the seeds of possibility. The mystery: we simply do not know what is potential within us. We can have only hints, tendencies, and others may have them too. The only way to know our potential is by fulfilling it.

The incredible violence, destruction, and pain of our day are crying out to us that we need a single minded and single hearted commitment to Life. Trying to explain her use of the grotesque in fiction, Flannery O'Connor said that when people are deaf you shout, and when they are blind you paint in bright colors. Reality is screaming at us that we have not paid sufficient and appropriate attention to our history and the deeper questions. We need to tell our stories and reflect on them. We need to ask our questions and set about seeking their answers. We need to engage ourselves in the inner processes that will help us to bring our memories and questions to the surface and follow them to the end, wherever they take us.

To do this requires a three-fold commitment. First, we must be oriented toward the truth, the reality of things as they are, the truth of God and ourselves and our human condition, in particular. But it is not enough to know the truth with our heads; we must also live it. Because the truth is often so difficult and demanding, hard to come by and hard to bear, our seeking must be motivated and sustained by love.

In western education, for too long the head and the heart have been disconnected. Unless the seed of truth in the head falls into the heart and takes root, that truth is lifeless. But it is equally true that if the truth of the heart is not expressed in some external form, that truth does not blossom. When the truth of the head is rooted in the heart, it becomes real, and when the truth of the heart is expressed through the head the world is transformed. If we are to move beyond ignorance and illusion, beyond control and denial, beyond the false dichotomies and lies that characterize our dysfunctional society, we must commit ourselves as individuals and as societies to living the truth in love.

As Thea Bowman sings so beautifully and demonstrates so compellingly with her life, "Done made my vow to the Lord. I will go. I shall go. To see what the end will be. Done opened my mouth to the Lord. And I never will turn back. I will go. I shall go. To see what the end will be. Sometimes I'm up, sometimes I'm down.

Done made my vow to the Lord, and I never will turn back. I will go. I shall go. To see what the end will be."

References

Aristotle (1954). *Poetics.* (I. Bywater, Trans.) New York: Modern Library.

Bauer, J. (1982). *Alcoholism and women: the background and the psychology.* Toronto: Inner City.

Benson, H., M.D. (1984) *Beyond the relaxation response: How to harness the healing power of your personal beliefs.* New York: Times.

Berry, T. (1987). *Thomas Berry and the new cosmology,* (A. Lonergan and C. Richards, Eds.) Mystic, Conn.: Twenty-third.

Bowman, T. (Vocalist). (1989). *Songs of my people* (Cassette recording). Boston: Krystal Records.

Clark, J.P.H. (1978). Sources and theology in *The cloud of unknowing. Downside Review,* 96, 281-98.

Craighead, M. (1987). Immanent mother, in M. Giles (Ed.) *The feminist mystic and other essays on women and spirituality* (pp. 71-83). New York: Crossroad.

Doran, R. M., S.J. (June, 1977). Aesthetics and the opposites, *Thought,* LII; Jungian psychology and Christian spirituality: I, II, and III (1979). *Review for Religious,* 38, 497-510; 742-752; 857-866.

Dossey, L. (1982). *Space, time & medicine.* Boston: Shambala.

Eliot, T.S. (1932). "Tradition and the individual talent," in *Selected Essays: 1931-1932,* pp. 3-11. New York: Harcourt.

Jung, C.G. (1959). *The archetypes and the collective unconscious. collected works,* Vol. 8, Princeton: Princeton UP; (1971) *Psychological types, collected works,* Vol. 6, Princeton: Princeton UP.

Koontz, Christian (1986). *Connecting: creativity and spirituality.* Kansas City: Sheed & Ward. Also *Evoked by the scriptures: keeping a scripture journal.* Kansas City: Sheed & Ward; (1990).

La Driere, J. (1956). "Structure, sound, and meaning," in *English Institute essays,* (N. Frye, Ed.) New York, 1956 (pp. 85-108).

Llewelyn, R. (1981, June 7). "The treatment of distractions in Zen and the *Cloud Of Unknowing." Fourteenth Century English Mystics Newsletter,* 2, 64-65.

Lonergan, B., S.J. (1972). *Method in theology.* New York: Seabury.

May, R. (1975). *The courage to create.* New York: Norton.

Morrison, T. (December, 1984). "Memory, creation, and writing." *Thought.* pp. 385-390.

Nolan, A. (1978). *Jesus before Christianity.* New York: Orbis.

Progoff, I. (1975). *At a journal workshop.* New York: Dialogue House; (1981). *The practice of process meditation,* New York: Dialogue House.

Rainer, T. (1978). *The new diary.* Los Angeles: Tarcher.

Rokeach, M. (1973). *The nature of human values.* New York: Free Press.

Schaef, A. (1987). *When society becomes an addict.* San Francisco: Harper.

Vargiu, J. (1977). Creativity. *Psychosynthesis 3-4: The Realization of the Self,* 17-53.

Weil, S. (1951). "Reflections on the right use of school studies with a view to the love of God," in *Waiting for God.* (pp. 105-116). New York: Harper.

Wilder, T. (1985). *The journals of Thornton Wilder (1939-1961).* (D. Gallup, Ed.), New Haven: Yale University Press.

Wolters, C. (Trans.) (1978). *The cloud of unknowing and other works.* New York: Penguin.